REMEMBERING IN VAIN

European Perspectives

European Perspectives
A Series in Social Philosophy and Cultural Criticism

Lawrence D. Kritzman and
Richard Wolin, Editors

European Perspectives seeks to make available works of inter-
disciplinary interest by leading European thinkers. By presenting classic texts and outstanding contemporary works,
the series hopes to shape the major intellectual controver-
sies of our day and thereby to facilitate the tasks of historical understanding.

REMEMBERING IN VAIN

The Klaus Barbie Trial and Crimes Against Humanity

Alain Finkielkraut

Translated by Roxanne Lapidus *with Sima Godfrey*

Introduction by Alice Y. Kaplan

Columbia University Press
New York

Columbia University Press
New York   Oxford
La Mémoire vaine. Du crime contre l'humanité copyright © 1989
Éditions Gallimard
Copyright © 1992 Columbia University Press
All rights reserved
Glossary compiled by Amy Allen and Alice Kaplan

Library of Congress Cataloging-in-Publication Data

Finkielkraut, Alain.
   [Mémoire vaine. English]
   Remembering in vain: the Klaus Barbie trial and crimes
against humanity / Alan Finkielkraut; translated by
Roxanne Lapidus with Sima Godfrey.
     p.   cm. — (European perspectives)
   Includes bibliographical references and index.
   ISBN 0-231-07464-6
   1. Barbie, Klaus, 1913– — Trials, litigation, etc. 2. War
crime trials — France — Lyon. 3. Holocaust, Jewish (1939–
1945) — France. 4. World War, 1939–1945 — France —
Lyon — Atrocities. I. Title. II. Series.
   JX5441.B37F56   1992
   341.6'9'0268445823 — dc20   92-19469
                                       CIP

Printed in the United States of America

c 10 9 8 7 6 5 4 3 2 1

In tribute to Primo Levi

Contents

Introduction

Alice Y. Kaplan

When the French press muses about who is going to replace
Sartre, Foucault, and Barthes in the pantheon of national intellectual figures, Alain Finkielkraut's name inevitably appears —
precociously — on a list that includes older, established figures
such as historian François Furet, sociologist Pierre Bourdieu,
philosophers Jacques Derrida and Gilles Deleuze, and writer-
psychoanalyst Julia Kristeva. Today's French intellectual, the
argument goes, is less grandiose, less oppositional, more interested in the analysis of discrete events than in global pro-
nouncements, a teacher and critic rather than a militant. Alain
Finkielkraut is difficult to place in any group. Some consider
him a liberal thinker in the newly minted French sense of the
term: antitotalitarian, anti-Marxist, devoted to the search for
universal values in a nation grappling with ethnic diversity (the
apparent points of convergence between this new French liber-
alism and American neoconservatism are not well understood).
Heideggerian in his metaphysics yet opposed to German romanticism, a secular disciple of Emmanuel Levinas, as well as a
Jewish intellectual engaging with the French literary tradition
(most recently with turn-of-the-century thinker Charles
Péguy), Finkielkraut appears to be one of a kind in his pen-
chants and positions. Culturally, he is a traditionalist: he priv-
ileges written over audiovisual culture, *belles lettres* over new
pedagogical method. He spoke out against the reform of
French spelling, and supported the gulf war. His academic
training is in literature; he is *agrégé* (meaning that he has passed

the extremely rigorous state exam making him a member of the teaching corps); he teaches literature at the Ecole Polytechnique, one of the highly competitive *Grandes Ecoles* that trains the French elite.

At age forty-four Alain Finkielkraut is the author of eleven books. Among them is a controversial reflection on Jewish identity, *Le Juif imaginaire* (The imaginary Jew; 1980), part autobiography, part politics, describing the dilemma of the affluent children of Holocaust survivors who sought their own political identity in the years following the student revolt of 1968. *L'Avenir d'une négation* (The future of a negation; 1982) is a response to Holocaust denial; Finkielkraut traces the anti-Semitism of the French left and the failure to come to terms with Nazi genocide. These books along with *Remembering in Vain* form a trilogy that places Alain Finkielkraut in a tradition with other children of World War II — Art Spiegelman in this country, Klaus Theweleit in Germany, the novelist Patrick Modiano in France — each a self-reflexive, self-critical theorist of memory.

In 1987, the year of the Klaus Barbie trial, Finkielkraut's *La Défaite de la pensée* (*The Defeat of Thought*; forthcoming from Columbia University Press in a revised edition) sparked a debate on the meaning of a national culture. It is at once a defense of the French enlightenment against German romanticism, a complaint about postcolonial politics, and an elite resistance in the face of mass culture. The book made Alain Finkielkraut a media figure. People searching to pigeonhole Finkielkraut have called him a "postjournalist" (in the sense that he takes the analysis of political debate a step beyond the news), an "enemy of relativism," or of romanticism, or of revisionism, depending on the context.

To understand the mood in which Alain Finkielkraut began to write about crimes against humanity in *Remembering in Vain*, it helps to see the image of him recorded by Marcel Ophuls in his documentary on Klaus Barbie, *Hotel Terminus*. Finkielkraut is emerging from the courtroom, standing on the courtroom steps. It's getting late and he is waiting for the verdict along with a large crowd. He is surrounded by cameras and he is looking into a camera. He is exhausted and he wears a sad smile. He starts to speaks slowly, carefully, and as he warms to his subject — as he gets angry — the words come faster:

> It's 10:30. We're waiting for the verdict. As for myself, I'm leaving this trial with a deepened sense of pessimism, first because I don't believe that the notion of *crimes against humanity* with which Barbie was charged has been adequately clarified by the trial. I think it was obscured, willfully by the defense, but also by the state, which did not know how to bring it to light and defend it properly. I think that throughout this trial we ought to have meditated, and even more than meditate, we should have been indignant over this situation in which a black man, an Arab, a Bolivian, and Vergès — a man who claims his Asian ancestry — rose to the defense of a Nazi, and furthermore that they defended him *in the name of* their race, in the name of their non-European identity.
>
> Imagine that we're in 1945, at the end of the war, and someone says, "you'll see, in twenty or thirty years when they accuse and condemn a Nazi torturer, it'll be the 'subhumans'" (that's what the Nazis called them) "who will defend him." Everyone would have laughed.

The elements of this speech — Finkielkraut's demand for clarification of "crimes against humanity," his outrage at the use of Third World rhetoric to defend a Nazi, and his sense of a pre-

sent so grotesque it would have been unthinkable in the past —
become the major themes of *La Mémoire vaine. Du crime contre
l'humanité,* published in France by the Editions Gallimard in
1989 and now available in this translation by Roxanne Lapidus
with Sima Godfrey.

In preparing an American audience to understand
Finkielkraut's view of the Barbie trial, it may be useful to signal
to the reader that Finkielkraut's positions relative to the trial are
at once speculative, idiosyncratic, and iconoclastic. His distrust
of multiculturalism will strike a reactionary note in the current
U.S. cultural context, although Finkielkraut's views — too
complex to be adapted by any party or platform — are not easily
assimilable to U.S. cultural conservatism of the kind that has
flourished in the Reagan-Bush years. Finkielkraut tends to see
historical causation from the "top down" (the top being sometimes philosophers, sometimes government or international
agencies) in a way that will not endear him to grass roots-
oriented social historians. It's bound to strike Americans as
wrong when he credits Nuremberg policy (rather than, say, the
southern black church) as a major factor in the U.S. civil rights
movement.[1] Finkielkraut's idealization of French political culture of the turn of the century is hard to grasp for those of us
who didn't grow up reading Péguy on Dreyfus. His bitterness
about the 1960s (which he refers to at one point as the CRS-SS
years — the years when people accused the French security police, the CRS, of being "as bad as the SS") is another deeply felt
issue we can only sense in passing here. Sometimes his writing
is so polemical — his rhetoric flames and jabs. But in his pages
on the return of the deportees, on the misuse of the word *Nazism*
in contemporary political jargon, on the distinction between the
resistance experience (*le monde*) and the Holocaust experience
(*l'immonde*), Finkielkraut is luminous.

As Americans, I think we have reason to be envious of Alain Finkielkraut, envious of his role as a thinker who can write for and be read by a large audience on a topic as difficult and abstract as jurisprudence. However disappointed Finkielkraut may have been about the Barbie trial, he attended it and took two years to investigate and criticize its legal and moral basis; his intellectual activism is worth emulating. We should also envy French intellectual life, which makes a place for an essay of this sort to be published by the country's major trade press and then debated in the daily newspapers.

There is already available in English a small but vital selection of work on Klaus Barbie that can be studied before or with Finkielkraut's essay. At the time of the Barbie trial, Jane Kramer's "Letter from Europe" in the *New Yorker* described the details of the trial and its cultural context with her usual pungency, sparing neither Barbie's defense lawyer nor Finkielkraut's *La Défaite de la pensée*.[2] Marcel Ophuls's documentary film on "the life and times of Klaus Barbie," *Hotel Terminus,* narrates Barbie's crimes, his life after the war, and his extradition, and includes a long conversation with one of the retired American intelligence officers who worked with Barbie, interviewed next to his swimming pool by Ophuls. Ted Morgan's *An Uncertain Hour* gives the longer cultural background from World War I leading up to Barbie's activity in Lyons.[3] Morgan, who grew up in France and only became an American citizen as an adult, narrates French culture from a uniquely double perspective. I recommend *An Uncertain Hour* as a companion to *Remembering in Vain* — especially the final chapter, "Last Train to Auschwitz," which reconstructs the story of the convoy of August 11, 1944 — deported on orders from Klaus Barbie — in its journey from Montluc prison to Auschwitz. Alain Finkielkraut's book, however, remains unique, because for him the Barbie trial is an occasion to articulate an ethics of memory.

Klaus Barbie was arrested in Bolivia in January 1983. At the close of World War II he was assisted in his flight out of Europe by American intelligence agents who signed him up for cold war espionage duty as an informer against communists. His "handlers" helped him to South America, where, since 1951, he had lived under the name Klaus Altmann. French Nazi hunters Serge and Beate Klarsfeld finally tracked him down in Bolivia. Over the years he appeared to have been involved with dictators, terrorists, and gun runners.

French President François Mitterand and his minister of justice, Robert Badinter, arranged for Barbie's extradition. He had already been tried twice in Lyons in absentia and sentenced to death for war crimes, but a statute of limitations annulled those sentences. And now there was no more death penalty in France; Robert Badinter, who abolished it, the same man who extradited Barbie, would not be able to preside over his execution. Badinter was the son of a man who had been deported to Auschwitz by Barbie in 1943 and died there.

Only a change in postwar French law allowed the French to try Barbie. In the mid-1960s, the French incorporated into French law a definition of "crimes against humanity" from the 1945 Nuremberg Trials, and at the time of the Barbie trial that definition was enlarged to include Barbie's crimes against the Resistance.[4] Crimes against humanity had no statute of limitations. One of the ensuing legal complexities of the Barbie trial was that thirty-nine different lawyers representing Jewish groups, Resistance groups, and individual survivors appeared in court to file a civil suit against Barbie; each lawyer delivered a separate deposition. Alain Finkielkraut is particularly critical of the blurring of crimes against humanity to include both deportation-related crimes and crimes against the Resistance, and part of his argument against the trial revolves around his sense of the different motives of these thirty-nine lawyers, the *parties civiles,* and the way tensions among them weakened the case against Barbie. One of the most moving aspects of his essay is the section devoted to explaining the difference between dying in an act of resistance — because one has chosen to fight — and dying for one's identity, dying, in the case of the Holocaust, simply for being a Jew.

Postwar history adds a further outrage even to the horror of the camps, the difficulty the French nation had in accepting the three thousand Jews who survived and who returned to France, often as displaced persons.[5] Jewish deportees who were tortured and sent to death camps by Barbie did not return to France as heroes but as embarrassing reminders of France's shame and guilt during the Occupation. For the resisters, who had chosen to fight, their struggle was aggrandized and made part of a myth of national resistance to Nazism. The returning deportees were not celebrated; they were "the zebra men," carrying in their tortured bodies the mark of France's collaborationist shame. Each group had witness to bear against Barbie, yet their history and motives were not the same. And yet the French court considered both to have been the victims of these refurbished "crimes against humanity."

The Barbie trial was not just a national event governed by national passions. It was also local. Barbie was being tried in Lyons, the major city of southeastern France, known for its silk trade, its Renaissance culture, and its three-star cuisine, because Lyons was where Klaus Barbie was stationed by the Gestapo and where he got the nickname "Butcher of Lyons." Barbie is best known in France for two acts. He was the murderer of

Jean Moulin, the greatest martyr of the French Resistance, arrested in Caluire (a suburb of Lyons) and tortured to death by Barbie in the Montluc prison. And he had sent forty-four Jewish children from their shelter in a children's home in Izieu (a small farming town east of the city) to death in the camps. Barbie was actually tried on forty-one separate counts of crimes against humanity. The torture and deportation of seven hundred and thirty Jews and resistants were attributed to him. A jury of nine citizens of Lyons found him guilty, and three judges from the Lyons criminal court sentenced him to life in prison.

The Barbie trial took place between May 11 and July 4, 1987. It was two years before the celebration of the bicentennial of the French Revolution and the Barbie trial was meant to be a pedagogical event. School children in the French system were given lessons about deportation during the Barbie trial. The newspapers and magazines were full of references to "memory," to "the lesson of history," to "an exemplary trial in service of human conscience." Columnists remarked regularly that the trial was as much an affair to be judged by philosophers and history professors as it was a matter for the courts. After much debate, the courtroom proceedings were discretely videorecorded and the videotapes put under lock and key until the year 2007. Although the trial itself was not available for viewing, *Shoah,* Claude Lanzmann's nine and a half hour documentary about the deportation of Polish Jews, was broadcast late at night on French television during the last days of the trial. Throughout the summer of 1987, the French press opened its columns to important figures from the war years. In the *Nouvel Observateur,* Simone Veil, president of the European Court and survivor of Auschwitz and Bergen-Belsen, worried that the trial would fail to confront the specificity of Nazism; the same weekly magazine published in the month of April a "guide to the collaboration," with capsule biographies of Brasillach, Céline, Henri Beraud, Drieu la Rochelle, Jean Luchaire, intellectuals who to one degree or another participated in collaborationist institutions. In May, *Le Monde* reprinted the text of the ignominious Jewish Statute of October 3, 1940, signed by Maréchal Pétain and his ministers, which denied Jews their public functions, stripped them of their professions, their civil service positions, their military status, etc. During Barbie's trial reminders of the war years were everywhere. The terrain had been prepared as early as 1983 by Jacques Vergès, Barbie's defense lawyer. Vergès had threatened in print and in public statements to reveal hypocrisy and betrayal within the ranks of the French Resistance. Former Resistance leaders rushed to protest. Lucie Aubrac, a former Resistance fighter whose husband had been arrested by Barbie along with Jean Moulin, decided to write her memoirs, which she published in 1984, using her BBC escape code phrase as her title, *Ils partiront dans l'ivresse* (Drunken, they'll go out).[6] Aubrac, a lifelong history teacher, wrote her memoir in the form of a *journal intime* — a diary — even though the events had happened forty-six years earlier. Her diary, in its technique, confirms one of Finkielkraut's notions about the Barbie trial: that it resuscitated history, made the past into a current event.

The Barbie trial was for France like an abreaction in psychoanalysis, a single relived piece of a trauma that brings the other buried pieces back to life. When abreaction works, it produces a catharsis and a cure. Finkielkraut would contend that the Barbie trial was the very opposite: that lots of time and work went into avoiding what should have been central; that with avoidance and denial came the release of accumulated social toxins.

Forty-three years had passed between Barbie's original

crimes and the trial itself. Many other things had happened to France, and to the world, since the Occupation; principal among them the loss of France's colonies during the national liberation struggles of the 1960s, the arrival of North African immigrants and the rise of a new anti-Semitism, anti-Arab racism, the drama of Israel and Palestine.

As early as 1955, Aimé Césaire, in a landmark speech on the evils of colonialism, had charged France with not being able to apply the lessons of World War II to its own racism in the subjugation of colonial peoples, with not being able to face the racism within themselves that had survived Hitler's death.[7] The analogy between Hitlerian racism and colonialist racism was painful and provocative and remained a rallying cry for French support of Algerian independence. Henri Alleg, a member of the Algerian communist party who was tortured by French generals, wrote a heartbreaking book about his own experience; the French officers who tortured him told him that they were using the same methods on him as had been used on them by the Gestapo when they were in the Resistance.[8] His book, *The Question*, was seized and banned by the government in 1958 and finally published, to great public outrage over the reality of French torture in Algeria. It is now widely read as testimony of a national tragedy. It is this very real history that makes Vergès's use of Algeria to defend Barbie so effective, and so cruelly manipulative.

Perhaps the most important single political event in France since the Second World War was the Evian accord of 1962, which made Algeria independent and brought to France thousands of *pieds noirs* — French who had lived in Algeria and now had to remake their lives in the French metropolis. At the same time, metropolitan France was transformed since the 1960s by the presence of a growing number of immigrants from North

Africa, and by anti-Arab racism. *S.O.S Racisme,* a kind of French rainbow coalition designed to support immigrant workers, organized an enormous rally at the Place de la Concorde in June of 1985; three hundred thousand people marched, wearing badges with the slogan "touche pas à mon pote" (don't hassle my immigrant friend). The political views of Jean-Marie Le Pen, leader of the National Front Party, express the post 1960s culture of reaction. Le Pen has said at various times in the past ten years that he would like to send the North African immigrants back to North Africa, that he would like to incarcerate victims of AIDS (*S.I.D.A.* in French — he called them "SIDAïques" a deliberate rhyme with *Judaïque*), and that the gas chambers were merely "a detail" of Second World War history. During the 1980s, Le Pen's popularity grew. Even though the Front National currently has no representatives in the French National Assembly, Le Pen himself garnered 14.4 percent of the popular vote in the first round of the 1988 presidential elections, coming in fourth overall.[9] Along with the rise of Le Pen, the 1980s are marked in France by what Vidal-Naquet calls "the paper Eichmanns," people who argue, in insanely pedantic, wrong-headed detail, that the gas chambers didn't exist and otherwise deny various established facts about the Holocaust.[10] They include Robert Faurisson (a former literature professor at Lyons) and Henri Roques, who sought a doctorate for his views. These crank theorists, descended from postwar fascists such as Maurice Bardèche, have come out of the woodwork. They have publishers and defenders on the extreme left and right and even a specialized book store in Paris. There can be no understanding of the French will to make the Barbie trials a commemorative event without feeling the intellectual and moral revulsion over what has become known as Holocaust negationism.[11]

The early 1980s are also marked, in France, by a series of terrorist bombings of public places: a Jewish delicatessen in 1982, an Orly Airlines counter in 1983, a department store frequented by North Africans in 1986. To complicate matters even further, a number of these bombings were claimed by a group demanding the release of Ibrahim Abdallah from French prison: Abdallah was in jail on charges of terrorism, and his lawyer was Jacques Vergès.

So the context in which Klaus Barbie was tried, while clearly marked by World War II history, was not the same as the context in which he had committed his crimes. And this simple fact turned out to have enormous consequences, which threatened the integrity of the trial. Vergès, a man with a mission to create moral discomfort, said France had no right to try Barbie because of France's own crimes in the colonies and because of Israel's crimes against the Palestinians. He evoked everything bad that had happened in the world since 1945, all the crimes of imperialism and state racism that had gone unpunished, thereby touching the nerves of people born after 1945, who are emotionally closer to those events than to World War II. He attempted to deflate the rhetoric surrounding the trial, accusing France of moral ineptitude and hypocrisy. If Alain Finkielkraut's own voice in *Remembering in Vain* is fraught with a rhetorical energy that comes from pent-up anger, it is because Vergès touched a nerve with a trick; he set up recent history in a competition with what had come before it.

The problem is not merely that forty-three years had passed since Barbie committed his crimes (that would make Vergès's position seem inevitable), but the way people understood those forty-three years and especially the way they construct analogies between one event and the next. Instead of connecting anti-Semitism with racism against non-Europeans, Vergès pits

Jews and non-Europeans against one another. Finkielkraut's analysis makes Vergès look cruel and triumphant. By some accounts Vergès's showmanship was received by the French in the summer of 1987 as buffoonery; he encouraged on the far right the worst kind of "France for the French" diatribes and became — ironically — the irritant that brought to the surface the same kind of racism he was so vociferously condemning.[12] Finkielkraut, in opposing Vergès, defends European values against Third World insensitivity, even though he would likely agree that European values contributed to the *shoah* and to today's anti-Semitism as surely as those values nourished colonialist racism. On either side of this debate, there appears to be no room both for facing the horror of the *shoah*, and for criticizing postwar European politics. Nothing inherent makes a discussion of colonialism cancel out a discussion of the *shoah*; nothing inherent makes a discussion of the *shoah* cancel out a discussion of the Third World. The political rift between two world perspectives is both tragic and emblematic of our times.

These twists and wrinkles of interpretation between 1945 and 1987 make the trial of Klaus Barbie a postmodern trial. Postmodern because it was forty-three years after the fact; postmodern because the man on trial seemed only a shadow version of the actual Butcher of Lyons (all that seemed to remain on his face of the horror he caused was a grimace, a "rictus" that the press would make much of); postmodern because his defense lawyer was defending him on the basis of history that occurred after his own crimes; postmodern because both the defense and the prosecutor were fragmented and even disagreed among themselves about which victims and what events they were representing. The defense wasn't talking about World War II; it was talking about colonialism and France's moral standing. The prosecution itself was divided between those speaking for the

Resistance heroes slaughtered by Barbie and those speaking for the Jews sent to die in extermination camps by Barbie. The Barbie trial was a postmodern trial because everything in it was at odds: the histories of the prosecuting groups, the motives of the defendant and defenders, the huge gap of time itself between the event and the trial.

For Finkielkraut, there is a trial that bears none of these flaws: Finkielkraut begins and ends *Remembering in Vain* by evoking a modern trial, that of Alfred Dreyfus. A French army colonel and an assimilated Jew, Dreyfus was framed at the turn of the last century for treason; incriminating papers later turned out to have been forged to look as though he had written them. His condemnation and exile to Devil's Island penitentiary, the ensuing protest, the discovery of a frame-up, and his retrial and redemption are lore. The Dreyfus trial was "modern" because it was utopian; it launched a certain righteous tradition of polemic that would have an effect on the world. His trial and retrial were causes célèbres, milked by a press that came into its own as a social force, some say, because of its effectiveness in saving Dreyfus. Another truism about the Drēyfus Affair is that it set up the basic political camps in France that lasted through World War II: Catholics and the army on the right; intellectuals and Jews on the left. From Finkielkraut's point of view, the story has a happy ending — the intellectuals won, and so did justice. The sovereignty of the army had been challenged by reason and individual rights. Here was justice lost and found through interpretation and protest. Finkielkraut doesn't quote the rhetoric of the Affaire Dreyfus itself but rather the memory of an old man who participated in it. That man was Charles Péguy, one of the most brilliant essayists in the pro-Dreyfus camp. In the passage cited by Finkielkraut on the first pages of *Remembering in Vain,* Péguy is writing about a young boy who had come to him to hear about the trial. In the moment of telling about the trial, Péguy realizes that the event he experienced has been frozen into history. He experiences the Dreyfus era, even as he is teaching it, as "embalmed." Péguy's view of history is pessimistic (already, according to Finkielraut, "postmodern"),[13] yet the relationship of past to present in Péguy's discourse on memory is still relatively clear. The present moves; the past remains still.[14] The Klaus Barbie story, by contrast, confuses decades, political positions, and moral stands. Historical agents from another era come back on the world stage to haunt what came after them. Inexplicable alliances ensue. Vergès, left-wing champion of Third World causes, is defending the right-wing Nazi and charging the socialist French state with political and moral hypocrisy. He is not defending his client so much as attacking the prosecution. The prosecution of Barbie must then become a defense against the defense. But it is divided, and can't speak with one voice. Péguy's student surely had something to learn from the Dreyfus Affair, embalmed though it may have been in Péguy's memory. In the case of the Barbie trial, what's the *use* of telling the story?

The point of the comparison between the Dreyfus trials and the Barbie trial isn't just about the unity of the Dreyfus narrative and the confusion of the Barbie narrative. In evoking the Dreyfus era, in longing for its clarity, Finkielkraut is also evoking a long tradition of essays and polemics in French writing, which began with Dreyfus and continues with Finkielkraut himself. Finkielkraut's essay is not merely a polemic, although it takes a strong position. Finkielkraut has taken the Barbie trial as an occasion to analyze an entire climate and set of philosophical problems facing a nation. In that sense, Finkielkraut's essay is as much a meditation as it is an argument. The writing moves from the specific moment and concrete descriptions to questions of community and the possibilities of memory and of justice. The range of allusions and quotations alone tells us something about Finkielkraut's imagination, about the way specifics speak for general truths. Finkielkraut ranges over the verdict of the Nuremberg war crimes trials, Primo Levi's memoir of Auschwitz (on the hell of not being believed), Pascal and Schopenhauer on humanity's understanding of its immortality, and the advertising slogan of a record store. Finkielkraut can switch from setting a scene to arguing a point of legal doctrine to the most angry polemical condemnations of a mentality or point of view.

Part of the density of his writing has to do with his love of paradox, which makes him a postmodern writer in spite of his philosophical abhorrence for postmodern confusion about what is right and what is relative. Among Finkielkraut's seemingly paradoxical maxims: 1) Barbie is important to try precisely because he was *unimportant* in the Nazi hierarchy (in combating a system that dehumanized humanity, it is vital to restore individual responsibility to each cog in the inhuman death machine); 2) Vergès misuses the analogy of Nazism so severely in his defense that everyone ends up sounding like a Nazi except the former Nazi himself; 3) "news" is the opposite of history and prevents us from remembering what happened.

Finkielkraut's arguments are so dense that it is hard to outline them without betraying their plasticity. Because of his sense of paradox, the truth can come out of the devil's mouth, as when Barbie himself, even as he denies his guilt, insists on the distinction between war crimes and crimes against humanity

("I never committed the roundup in Izieu. I never had the power to decide on deportations. I fought the Resistance, which I respect, with toughness, but that was war and the war is over").[15] And Finkielkraut is not easily satisfied, even with his own suggestions. "Universalism," which he might seem to suggest as a condition for true justice, comes under scrutiny, because we have no examples of universal thinking that don't tend toward the totalitarian; Finkielkraut condemns the proliferation of analogies that trivialize the memory of Nazism (so and so are "as bad as the Nazis"), but nonetheless insists that it is wrong-headed to view the Holocaust as a *unique* historical event. If it can only happen once, what is the point of legislation concerning crimes against humanity?

Finkielkraut believes in the law, finally, and he believes in it as a defense against the relativism of ideology. He suggests the importance of a *place* where the states of the world would be responsible for their actions. Does this place already exist? Is it a court? The U.N. security council? The World Court? The Reagan administration was put on trial in the World Court for mining the harbors of Nicaragua. The tribunal gave an anti-United States judgment; Reagan refused to accept it.[16] World law only works if world leaders will recognize it.

Finkielkraut's real opponent in *Remembering in Vain* is, however, not an imperfect legal system or even Klaus Barbie himself; it is Barbie's defense attorney Jacques Vergès. Of course, Vergès never went up against Finkielkraut in the courtroom, but Finkielkraut takes him on in this book as though they were direct adversaries. The contrast between Vergès's and Finkielkraut's thinking and polemics couldn't be greater.

Vergès is the product of a mixed colonial marriage, Vietnamese and French; his French father lost his civil service position for marrying a Vietnamese woman; the dismissal was the beginning of a suspicion toward French institutions that has dominated Vergès's life. Vergès made his reputation in the 1960s as a lawyer for the FLN, the Algerian nationalist movement. Finkielkraut, on the other hand, is a self-described affluent child of Holocaust survivors who wanted to indulge him because their life had been so hard. He is suspicious of his own generation's identification in the 1960s with Third World causes, and he wants the memory of the Holocaust protected by the law.

Vergès is the perfect enemy for Finkielkraut because he mistrusts the law and seeks to confuse it. Vergès wants a Pandora's box version of crimes against humanity, where one crime calls up all the others and makes them intolerable — puts them into competition with each other so that justice is always hypocritical. Finkielkraut wants a containable version of crimes against humanity, containable via the law, so that each crime can be dealt with in and of itself without entering into competition or analogy with the others.

Finkielkraut is the writer who looks to the law for justice, and Vergès is the lawyer who looks to the media to destroy the law. Two world views: Finkielkraut wants to build an ethics; Vergès wants to unsettle one. Vergès is situational, subversive; Finkielkraut is Kantian, rule-bound.

In defending Barbie, Vergès's strategy was to focus national attention on the Resistance. He promised to reveal internal disloyalty and treason within the French Resistance movement, and to prove that Jean Moulin, its leader, had not been tortured to death by Barbie but was rather betrayed by a Frenchman and committed suicide in despair. Although no evidence supporting his theory was ever revealed, the strategy itself was corrosive. The issue of deportation and genocide was in danger of being lost in all the media attention given to the Resistance plot. Finkielkraut argues — angrily — in *Remembering in Vain* that although Barbie was found guilty, Vergès won the trial (again, the trope is paradox). He won because he captured the imagination of the media, and because the world is more interested in the media than in justice. Finkielkraut claims that Vergès was admired by the press for internationalizing the issues; Barbie shook hands with the African lawyers; Vergès claimed this was a sign that Barbie was no longer a racist. The press ate it up.

When Finkielkraut attacks the media during the Barbie trial, he is attacking Vergès as a creature of the media, or rather he is attacking the media as Vergès's creature.

Vergès also furnishes Finkielkraut a wealth of anecdotal evidence on which to wage an attack on moral relativism, an issue which has informed much of Finkielkraut's previous work. In Finkielkraut's view of the Barbie trial as a moral failure, some lesser issue is always canceling out the greater one; guilt is always displaced by sentimentalism or show business or hypocrisy; interest groups are always competing for attention instead of attending to the truth.

Alain Finkielkraut spent two years after the Barbie trial reading about crimes against humanity. He read Hannah Arendt on the Eichmann trial. He read the transcripts of the International Military Tribunal at Nuremberg, and he read the London Charter that set up the conditions for the trial. He read Primo Levi's memories of Auschwitz and the return from Auschwitz. Primo Levi, a writer who proved that it was not only possible but essential to create poetry after Auschwitz, committed suicide the spring before the Barbie trial; *Remembering in Vain* is dedicated to his memory and his loss is at its center. The

Finkielkraut who, in *Remembering in Vain,* describes the arbitrary cruelty of racial deportation and demands justice is a more mature, outward-looking writer than the Finkielkraut of *Le Juif imaginaire* (1980), strident and even self-incriminating in his need to come to terms with the difference between his own relatively coddled condition and his parents' experience of Auschwitz. That immeasurable gap between two generations, much more than a generation gap, is, in both books, at the core of Finkielkraut's will to remember, the energy he writes from.

But what does Finkielkraut want? He wants a universal court of law, but he mistrusts transcendent thinking. He wants memory, but he mistrusts the news media, which trivialize history. He wants the Barbie trial to have been like the Dreyfus Affair, where guilt and innocence were clearly demarcated by dedicated, clear-thinking writers and jurists. He doesn't want the Barbie trial turned into another television show. Finkielkraut wants the law to be responsible for memory and for safeguarding humanity against the possibility of its own destruction. He figured out some of the defects in the London Charter that established protocol for Nuremberg (the fact, for example, that crimes against humanity, by definition, have to have been committed during wartime), and yet he holds up the Nuremberg Trials as a model of international accountability. Here is Finkielkraut's most essential formulation: we once thought that individuals died, but humanity itself continued unimpaired. The Holocaust taught us that humanity itself is mortal. The notion of crimes against humanity is the juridical trace of the coming to consciousness of humanity's mortality, the legal protection that is going to safeguard what law for individuals can't do. Finkielkraut wants crimes against humanity to be defined, clarified, and ready and waiting to protect humanity.

In Alain Finkielkraut's critique of television at the end of *Remembering in Vain,* an apple keeps appearing. Someone is eating an apple in front of a television set. For Finkielkraut, the apple signifies distraction from the truth. (It is undignified to sit in front of a box and eat while deportees testify about their torture.) The apple, as Finkielkraut well knows, couldn't be a more exemplary image; the apple stands for the fruit eaten by Adam and Eve that got us sent out of the garden of Eden and out of innocence. It is the fruit of knowledge and sin — both truth and the possibility of lying. That World War II is going to be represented, and misrepresented, is as inevitable as life outside Eden.

Because the Barbie trial did become a media event, it had the weakness of the media; it was sentimentalized and trivialized, distorted and valued for the wrong reasons. And because it was a media event, it penetrated French national consciousness. If you went to the dentist in June or July 1987, you talked about the Barbie trial. If you went to the coiffeur, you talked about the Barbie trial, if you read the newspapers, you read about the Barbie trial; and if you sat at the family dinner table, chances are you talked about the Barbie trial, whether you lived in low income housing in the northern suburbs of Paris or in a chateau in Sologne. The Barbie trial was an event of major cultural importance, whose process, finally, was as important as its result. It has influenced the teaching of French history, it has challenged French jurisprudence, and it has affected every debate about politics and culture to have come in its wake.

The Barbie trial has had ramifications for the way the French understand the relationship of World War II to the Algerian War, the two major traumas of contemporary France. If Vergès's defense was grotesque, it also forced people to think about the two events at the same time — two national secrets, two sources of pain and confusion and shame.

Why should Americans be interested in the Barbie trial at all? There are the obvious reasons, which transcend national perspective: the importance of commemorating Nazi genocide and the prophylactic and ethical necessity of historical memory. France has been marred by negationism but so has the United States. We have our own burgeoning industry of neo-Nazi groups and Holocaust deniers.[17] And we have our own never-resolved, escalating problems of racism and immigration.

Our recent national leaders are known, or should be known, for their insensitivity to the historical record. Our Vice President Dan Quayle, in one of the faux pas for which he is justly famous, was asked about the Holocaust and replied by calling it "an obscene period in our nation's history." He then corrected himself by saying, "Not our nation's but in World War II. I mean we all lived in this century. I didn't live in this century but in this century's history."[18] The quotation is only a malapropism, an intellectual stutter, but it still makes for a mad sort of epigraph to the American translation of *La Mémoire vaine,* adding home-grown evidence to Finkielkraut's diagnosis of a civilization incapable of thinking historically.

There is a more concrete reason for Americans to be interested in the trial of Klaus Barbie, and that is because his escape from justice after the war was our doing.

In 1983, Allan A. Ryan, Jr., issued a Justice Department report examining the U.S. relationship with Barbie.[19] Army officials in the counterintelligence corps had lied to U.S. civilian authorities, who then lied unwittingly to the French about Barbie's whereabouts. The counterintelligence personnel had lied because they were employing Barbie as an anticommunist informant. Because they lied, Barbie escaped extradition to France. Eventually the army paid "the rat line," an underground that transported communist defectors and U.S. intelligence informants out of Europe, to get Barbie out of harm's way. The "rat line" arranged for Barbie to get a passport and a Bolivian visa under the name Klaus Altmann, and put him and his family on a ship out of Genoa in 1951.

There was no reason to believe that these American army officials knew about Barbie's complicity in deporting Jewish civilians, nor any evidence that they made any special effort to learn about his actions. Barbie had described himself to them, just as he would describe himself to the Lyonnais court in 1986, as someone who had been in charge of combating the Resistance. Maybe U.S. intelligence officers read about Barbie's crimes in the press, maybe not. In any case, if we can generalize about "mentalities" based on Marcel Ophuls's interviews in *Hotel Terminus*, the French Resistance, in the eyes of American counterintelligence circa 1950, was tainted by "communism" and had therefore been a menace to the Free World. The use of Barbie, a former Gestapo officer, could be justified in cold war terms.

Allan Ryan's Justice Department report on Barbie, neither apologetic nor vindictive, has a lucid calm and a sad wisdom one doesn't expect in a government document; the sadness it exudes, in particular, comes from the unveiling of an American intelligence bureaucracy that is not so much wrong as it is naive and entirely ignorant of its own criminality.

In a cover letter to his report, Ryan sums up the consequences of the American actions, and he specifically addresses the problem of "time out of whack" in the Barbie trial: "It is a principle of democracy and the rule of law that justice delayed is justice denied. If we are to be faithful to that principle — and we should be faithful to it — we cannot pretend that it applies only within our borders and nowhere else. We have delayed justice in Lyons."[20]

After the publication of the Ryan report, the U.S. government sent a note to the French embassy expressing "deep regrets" for having concealed Barbie.

Klaus Barbie was condemned to life in prison by the French on the fourth of July.

In the year 2007, the videotapes of the Klaus Barbie trial will be made available to the public by the French government. Still another time gap will exist, between the events, the trial, and the viewing of the trial. The people who testified will be dead. Other unforeseen events will have further altered the world stage. What will the young people think? Who will lead the debate on the meaning of these buried tapes? It is good that Finkielkraut's book will be there. He has raised the important problems: the denial and the distortion of history with the passing of time, the problem of justice in a media age, the mortality of humanity itself. Whatever has changed in 2007, the issues he raises will still be vital as long as there are people around to raise them. There is also something in Finkielkraut's writing, at the level of his style, that makes me think *Remembering in Vain* will continue to be read, not just for a sense of the Barbie trial but for an understanding of postmodern history. I suspect it is the way Finkielkraut uses paradox, the way he creates intrigue and challenges the reader's sense of logic, the way his rhetoric moves us along in a kind of appalled fascination with humanity that makes him a convincing spokesman, a *porte-parole* for his times.

Notes

---

*With special thanks to Linda Orr and her Spring
1990 seminar in French Literature and History for
inviting me to join their discussion of* La mémoire
vaine. *David Auerbach, Cathy N. Davidson, H. D.
Harootunian, Cynthia Herrup, Lawrence Kritzman, Joseph Levine, Kristin Ross, Jane Tompkins,
and Marianna Torgovnick read early drafts of this
essay; I am grateful for their comments. Amy Allen
provided valuable research assistance.*

1. On the early phases of the civil rights movement, see William Henry Chafe, *Civilities and Civil Rights: Greensboro, North Carolina, and the Black Struggle for Freedom* (New York: Oxford University Press, 1980), Steve Lawson, *Running for Freedom: Civil Rights and Black Politics in America Since 1941* (Philadelphia: Temple University Press, 1991), and Taylor Branch, *Parting the Waters: America in the King Years 1954–1963* (New York: Simon and Schuster, 1988).

2. Jane Kramer, "Letter from Europe," *New Yorker*, October 12, 1987.

3. Ted Morgan, *An Uncertain Hour: The French, the Germans, the Jews, the Klaus Barbie Trial, and the City of Lyon, 1940–1945* (New York: William Morrow, 1990).

4. See Arnaud Lyon-Caen, "De Nuremberg au procès Barbie," in *Le Procès Nuremberg: conséquences et actualisation* (Bruxelles: Editions Bruylant, Editions de l'Université de Bruxelles, 1988), pp. 47–65. The original French law incorporating the Nuremberg definition of crimes against humanity dates from December 26, 1964.

5. The statistic is from Michael Marrus and Robert Paxton, *Vichy France and the Jews* (New York: Basic Books, 1981), p. 344, cited by

Judith Friedlander, *Vilna on the Seine: Jewish Intellectuals in France since 1968* (New Haven: Yale University Press), p. 28. See Marrus and Paxton for the history of French Jews during the Occupation.

6. Lucie Aubrac, *Ils partiront dans l'ivresse: Lyon: mai 1943; Londres: février 1944* (Paris: Le Seuil, 1984).

7. Aimé Césaire, *Discours sur le colonialisme* (Paris: Présence Africaine, 1955).

8. Henri Alleg, *La Question* (Paris: Editions de Minuit, 1961).

9. Statistic courtesy the Cultural Services branch of the French Embassy, New York.

10. Pierre Vidal-Naquet, *Assassins of Memory: Essays on the Denial of the Holocaust*, foreword and translation by Jeffrey Mehlman (New York: Columbia University Press, 1993).

11. See Alain Finkielkraut, *L'Avenir d'une négation. réflexion sur la question du génocide* (Paris: Le Seuil, 1982) and Pierre Vidal-Naquet, *Assasins of Memory: Essays on the Denial of the Holocaust*, foreword and translation by Jeffrey Mehlman (New York: Columbia University Press, 1992). On Revisionism in an international context, see Gill Seidel, *The Holocaust Denial: Antisemitism, Racism, and the New Right* (Leeds: Beyond the Pale Collective, 1986).

12. I am indebted to Françoise Melzer for this perspective.

13. In his response to a draft of this essay, March 1992, Finkielkraut quotes Péguy on the gap between history and reality: "Je lui donnais du réel, il recevait de l'histoire" ("A Nos Amis, A Nos Abonnés," *Oeuvres en Prose 1909–1914*, Gallimard, Editions de la Pléiade, 1957, p. 46). Péguy is not optimistic about the pedgagoical opportunity created by the telling of the Dreyfus Affair. "He shows," Finkielkraut writes, "that history has, in a sense, *vanquished* memory."

14. For Finkielkraut's extended analysis of Péguy as "reader of the modern world" see his *Le Mécontemporain: Péguy, lecteur du monde moderne* (Paris: Gallimard/nrf, 1992).

15. Finkielkraut *Remembering in Vain*, p. 24. Finkielkraut's source for Barbie's statement of July 3, 1987 is a special issue of *Le Monde* entitled *Le Procès de Klaus Barbie*, published separately in July 1987.

16. The World Court vote favoring Nicaragua took place May 10, 1984. In January 1985, the United States rejected the World Court decision.

17. In the fall of 1991, the Duke University student newspaper, *The Chronicle*, published a paid advertisement from a group claiming to be bringing the "good news" of Holocaust denial. Northwestern University, the University of Michigan, and Cornell University were also targeted for the ad.

18. Quoted by Elizabeth Drew, in the *New Yorker*, October 10, 1988, p. 102.

19. *Klaus Barbie and the United States Government: A Report to the Attorney General of the United States*, submitted by Allan A. Ryan, Jr. (Washington, D.C.: U.S. Department of Justice, Criminal Division, August 1983).

20. Quoted in the *New York Times*, August 17, 1983, p. 1, column 1.

Further Reading in English

Hannah Arendt, *Eichmann in Jerusalem: A Report on the Banality of Evil* (New York: Penguin, 1964). Philosopher Hannah Arendt's account of the Eichmann trial.

Jean-Denis Bredin, *The Affair: The Case of Alfred Dreyfus*, tr. Jeffrey Mehlman (New York: Braziller, 1986). Excellent synthesis of the Dreyfus affair by a French lawyer.

Marguerite Duras, *The War: A Memoir*, tr. Barbara Bray (New York: Pantheon, 1986). Especially part 1, on her husband's return from Belsen and his return to life.

Judith Friedlander, *Vilna on the Seine: Jewish Intellectuals in France Since 1968* (New Haven: Yale University Press, 1990). Contains a capsule biography and intellectual profile of Alain Finkielkraut.

Primo Levi, *If This is a Man* and *The Truce*, tr. Stuart Woolf (New York: Viking Penguin, 1979). Philip Roth called this memoir of Auschwitz and after "one of the century's truly necessary books."

xxxv

Michael Marrus and Robert Paxton, *Vichy France and the Jews* (New

York: Basic Books, 1981). French anti-Semitic policy during the Occupation in tandem and distinct from Nazi policy.

Ted Morgan, *An Uncertain Hour: The French, the Germans, the Jews, the Klaus Barbie Trial, and the City of Lyon, 1940–1945* (New York: William Morrow, 1990). French cultural history from World War I to the Occupation; Barbie's actions and their consequences.

Bradley F. Smith, *Reaching Judgment at Nuremberg* (New York: Basic Books, 1977). A concise study of the trials, from the perspective of the bench, aimed at the general reader.

Telford Taylor, *Nuremberg and Vietnam: An American Tragedy* (Chicago: Quadrangle Books, 1970). Former American prosecutor at Nuremberg applies Nuremberg principles to the American involvement in Vietnam.

Gill Seidel, *The Holocaust Denial: Antisemitism, Racism, and the New Right* (Leeds: Beyond the Pale Collective, 1986). Negationism in France, England, and the United States.

Robert K. Woetzel, *The Nuremberg Trials in International Law* (New York: Praeger, 1960). The most complete discussion available in English of the international legal aspects of the Nuremberg trials.

Remembering in Vain

CHAPTER ONE

HISTORY'S LAST
SUMMONS

In an article in *Cahiers de la Quinzaine* written in 1909, Péguy
tells of the visit of a young man, a boyish eighteen-year-old, who
came to question him about the Dreyfus Affair, which, as we
know, was the great event of Péguy's life:

> He was so docile. He had his hat in his hand. He kept turning it
> around with his fingers. He listened and listened to me. He
> drank in my words. *He was becoming informed. He was learning.*
> Alas, he was learning history. He was being instructed. Never
> had I understood so well as then, never had I sensed so instanta-
> neously, as in a flash, what history was; I felt the unbridgeable
> abyss that exists, that lies gaping between the real event and the
> historic event; I felt the complete and absolute incompatibility,
> the total strangeness, the lack of communication, the incom-
> mensurability between them — that is, the literal absence of any
> possible common means of measure. . . . Never had I seen in
> such a flash, so overwhelmingly, that there is the present and
> there is the past. The present — however long — in which people
> move. The past — however far it has already reached, however
> much it advances, however high it rises, wherever it has already
> triumphed . . . — where people do not move, and where people
> have good reason not to move.[1]

1

With the Barbie trial, it was the reverse situation that we experienced. While Péguy saw history assimilate the Dreyfus Affair — embalming and shelving it with relentless deference alongside other famous trials — we were able to see an already historical past transmuted into a judiciary present. For two months at the Palais de Justice in Lyons, within the framework of a criminal debate, protagonists from an era believed bygone reclaimed their story from the historians. By focusing our attention on the sentence and no longer simply on knowledge or on commemoration, this judiciary ceremony filled in the abyss that had separated us from the era of Barbie and his victims. The very fact that we waited along with them for the verdict made us their contemporaries. What had happened more than forty years ago was receiving today, before our eyes, its epilogue.

"For every man and every event," wrote Péguy, again, "there comes a moment, an hour; an hour strikes when they become historic; a certain stroke of midnight sounds on a certain village clock tower when the real event passes over into history."[2]

The Barbie trial reminded us that this stroke of midnight had not yet sounded, entirely, for the Holocaust, in spite of passing time, in spite of knowledge that has accrued, and in spite of the many works that fortunately continue to accumulate.

It was said — perhaps prematurely — of this trial that it provided a great lesson in history for the younger generation. On the contrary, its value comes entirely from the will — expressed and accomplished by the court — to snatch back (perhaps for the last time) Nazi crimes from the shroud of history.

CHAPTER TWO

THE LEGALITY
OF EVIL

But was Barbie worth the trouble? Was it necessary, in the interest of teaching a lesson or of delaying the fatal deadline of historicization, to pursue and judge forty years (two generations!) later the acts of this paltry underling, this monstrous subaltern, this poor man's Eichmann? What, in fact, is the chief of sections 4 and 6 of the Sipo-SD security police of Lyons in comparison to the great Nazi dignitaries who appeared at Nuremberg, at Frankfurt, or in Jerusalem? Not much, no doubt, but this objection — often expressed about the Barbie trial — is nonetheless not acceptable. For it misses the main point. From the top of the ladder to the bottom, from Eichmann to the engineers on the trains, the Final Solution was a crime of employees. Bureaucrats or policemen, civilians or soldiers, its protagonists were all underlings who did their job and who were under orders. No matter what their rank in the hierarchy of the state, the mainsprings of their actions were competence and obedience. As Max Picard wrote immediately after the war:

> That is what is new and terrifying about Nazi cruelty. It is no longer on a human scale, but on a scale that falls outside the hu-

3

man, on a par with laboratory apparatus or industrial machinery. Even the cruelty of Nero and of Caligula at least maintained a link with the men they were, with their brutal flesh and their perverted sensuality; one could still recognize in the crime the wreckage of the man. Nazi cruelty emanated from an industrial apparatus or from a man transformed entirely into apparatus.[1]

An industrial apparatus itself nationalized, integrated into the apparatus of the state. As demonstrated in great depth by Edgar Faure, France's adjunct prosecutor at the international tribunal at Nuremberg, the German Reich had erected a veritable "criminal public service" that organized its murderous activities "according to the administrative methods by which other states carry out their regular functions."[2]

It was precisely to remove from *crime* the excuse of *service* and to restore the quality of *killers* to law-abiding citizens "brought up with good principles and repulsed by the sight of torture"[3] — yet who worked to bring it about — that the category of "crimes against humanity" was formulated, between 1942 and 1945. The members of the exterminating bureaucracy did not in fact make war. (From Nuremberg onward, Edgar Faure defined the Nazi "treatment" of the Jewish Question as a *gratuitous crime* totally detached from the necessities and horrors of the military enterprise.) But at the same time, it was impossible to judge them as vulgar common-law criminals:

> If the expression "common-law crime" has a precise meaning, this meaning presumes a revolt by the delinquent against the forces representing the social order in which he is acting. Now, the crimes of the Nazi leaders present precisely this singularity, of having been committed in conformity with an order, in the very exercise of those forces.[4]

To the singular crime, the specific offense: thus there appeared alongside the crime against peace, the war crime and the "criminal exercising of personal power" that is common-law crime, "crimes against humanity" — "the criminal exercising of the power of the state."[5] This was a momentous judicial event, and yet the Allies had invented nothing. By referring, beyond the diversity of concrete laws, to eternal principles — to laws of humanity applicable to all nations — the judges at Nuremberg were following the classical tradition of the Rights of Man that Montesquieu defined as "the civil code of the Universe, in the sense that every people is a citizen thereof."[6] Furthermore, they reclaimed for their own use the first article of faith of the Enlightenment, that is, the affirmation of a morality holding "for nations and for individuals, for sovereigns and subjects, for the government official and for the obscure citizen."[7] This universalism had never been able to descend from the heights of theory, it is true, for it had always collided with another founding principle of modern politics — the absolute sovereignty of the state. Was it not by invoking a law superior to the state that religious fanaticism had plunged sixteenth-century Europe into total political chaos? And since God was now out of the picture, was there not the risk of reanimating the crusading spirit, of returning to anarchy, this time in the name of great humanitarian principles? In short, before Nuremberg, European thought was tugged back and forth between two contradictory postulations. While the idealists, for their part, called upon universal conscience to see that the rights of humanity were respected in all circumstances, the realists, having emerged from the experience of the wars of religion, favored protecting international order from the impulses — generous or self-interested — of a morality of conviction. On one hand, judicial humanism advanced

5

the idea of *jus gentium*, to the point of achieving, at the International Peace Conference at The Hague in 1907, the signing of the International Convention on Laws and Customs of War. On the other hand, political realism treated this declaration of the rights and duties of warring nations as dead prose by depriving it of all powers of punishment. Thus, after the end of the First World War, and in spite of the Treaty of Versailles, which obliged the German government to hand over all persons accused of war crimes, a list of which would be provided, the allied powers resigned themselves in the end to letting Germany itself organize the crackdown, and the majority of the accused were acquitted in the Leipzig trials.

For the rest, that is, for the crimes of state which were not specifically war crimes, a policy of noninterference prevailed and the retributive zeal that had been inspired by the idea of laws of humanity passed before having even generated any changes in the law. To be sure, in 1915 the governments of France, Great Britain, and Russia, deeply shocked by the Turkish treatment of the Armenian question, publicly advised the Sublime Portal (the Ottoman government) that the deportation and murder of Armenian nationals constituted "crimes against humanity and civilization," and that "all of the members of the Ottoman government as well as its agents found implicated in such massacres would be held personally responsible for the aforesaid crimes."[8] But in spite of the defeat of Turkey, which had entered the war aligned with Germany, this solemn protestation was not followed through — no tribunal was set up to judge the Turkish Youth Brigade, nor were their activities condemned as illegal. *Cujus regio, ejus religio:* to every state its own religion, its own system of justice, its own police and its own morality.

Thus it was only after World War II, with its unheard-of ros-

ter of monstrosities, that the laws of humanity entered into concrete law, and that their violation, like that of the laws of war,
was punished for the first time. Two reasons for this (relative)
intrepidness: the breadth of the cataclysm, that is, the *intrusion
of these crimes* in every country of Occupied Europe, and the meticulousness of the Nazis — the falsification of morality by reg-
ulation, of the legitimate by the legal, of ethical rigor by disciplinary rigidity. Since the normative power of legality could go
as far as to reverse the commandment "Thou shalt not kill!" by
commanding participation in a "criminal public service," this
evil had to be fought on its own ground, through the creation of
a higher legality. Since *forgetting* the laws of humanity — in the
satisfaction of one's duty accomplished or in one's sense of
professionalism — could prove to be even more murderous than
their transgression, it was necessary to confer upon those laws a
mode of existence henceforth unforgettable. Edgar Faure
wrote in 1947:

> Of course there will always be men with fanatical thoughts or
> with the drive to torture, but what we can avoid, what we can
> prevent, is that capital, discipline, and technology come to sub-
> ordinate an economy, an army, and an administration in the ser-
> vice of some new fanaticism. For the criminal genius of the fu-
> ture, no doubt this will have merely the effect of information and
> of precaution perhaps to be exercised, but it could be heeded by
> the average man who is an accomplice by weakness, by spine-
> lessness, or by a false interpretation of his duty to his country.
> That man will have to learn to reflect and to "imagine" the possi-
> ble consequences of the acts he commits in the course of his pro-
> fessional work. He must conceive of moral values and a justice
> superior to the state authority to which he is subject. No doubt
> enlightened people are already familiar with the subordination
> of the temporal to the spiritual, but for so many others, it is im-

7

portant that justice, not just abstract justice, but practical justice — courts, sentences, punishments — be elevated, for once, above the power of the state, not only of the criminal state but of victim states that have abdicated their power to punish in favor of an organization that goes beyond them.[9]

An average man become a little torturer, Barbie was no doubt only an underling, a small cog in the huge Nazi death machine. And his defense lawyer rightly stressed "the extreme modesty"[10] of his position, his role, his career and his rank. All the more reason to respect Beate and Serge Klarsfeld's determination to find Barbie and to have him prosecuted by a tribunal! The argument of his insignificance, far from invalidating the trial, is its primary justification. With regard to Nazi cruelty taken as a whole, the executioners, taken one by one, all appear insignificant, since this cruelty "is no longer on a human scale, but on a scale that falls outside the human." And the meaning, the scope — both ontological and judiciary — of the notion of crime against humanity is, precisely, to reestablish the link between the man and the crime, a link broken by the technical-administrative machine; to recall, by treating the *cogs* in the Nazi apparatus as *persons*, that service to the state does not exonerate any civil servant in any bureaucracy, nor any engineer in any laboratory, from his responsibility as an individual.

CHAPTER THREE

THE QUID PRO QUO

There is therefore no reason to regret that Klaus Barbie was wrested, even in extremis, from the tranquility of his Bolivian retreat to be delivered into the hands of justice. On the other hand, what one might have legitimately deplored (but who did?) was the absence of an international jurisdiction to rule on his case.

If in fact the crimes for which Barbie had to answer attack, as their name indicates, all of humanity, the judgment should have been rendered by a tribunal speaking in the name of the human race. This reasoning, which was that of the Allies in 1945, led the philosopher Karl Jaspers in 1961 to ask the tribunal in Jerusalem before which Eichmann was appearing to declare itself incompetent. At the end of that trial, Hannah Arendt wrote that the State of Israel should, instead of executing the sentence, "present" its prisoner to the United Nations — an unwieldy gift, to be sure, which would have provoked "quite an uproar," but one that it was necessary to make in order to prevent the world community from washing its hands of Eichmann — to remind it that the will to wipe out a particular race had attacked all — and to avoid contributing, itself, to reducing the impact of the Nazi enterprise: "The very monstrousness of the

9

events is 'minimized' before a tribunal that represents one nation only."[1]

It is true that Barbie, unlike Eichmann, perpetrated most of his crimes in one particular country. The Declaration on the Atrocities, signed August 30, 1943, in Moscow by the Soviet Union, the United States, and Great Britain, stipulated that this type of criminal activity came under the judicial and legislative competence of the country wronged, and that the only persons needing to be punished "by a common decision of the allied governments" were those criminals whose crimes "were without precise geographic localization."[2] But this objection is not valid for the trial in Lyons. Since the statute of limitations for the majority of his purely local activities had run out, Barbie was handed over to a French court in 1987 for his role in the deportation of Jews and members of the Resistance — that is, in a criminal proceeding that was not limited to French territory. If France has just experienced its first trial for crimes against humanity, it is, in fact, for want of an international criminal justice system.

This time no one gets worked up about it. And yet, what a fiasco! First of all, it is not humanity that is judging and punishing the Nazis, but simply their victims. Second and moreover, the other "criminal public service" branches have nothing to fear from the law. The Kantian program of an "international justice based on the rights of man"[3] was never realized: no superior authority, no international organization today dissuades the common man from lending his strength and support to nationalized crime. The Armenians are still fighting, seventy years after the fact, for international recognition of their genocide; the campaign against the Kulaks in the Ukraine is considered a crime against humanity only in the novels of Vassili Grossmann or Vassil Barka; the massacres in Bangladesh and the Biafran genocide moved out of the headlines only to founder in total oblivion. As for the Khmer Rouge, although defeated and ousted from power by the Vietnamese, they continue to hold a seat at international proceedings with total impunity, under the name of the Democratic Kampuchea.

In short, it is national jurisdictions today that apply the category of "crimes against humanity" to the Nazis — and to them alone. Which means that once the last followers of the Third Reich disappear the charge will fall into disuse, without, however, the criminal practice itself having been abandoned.

Far from being affected by this powerlessness, many Jews and friends of Jews see in it a tribute paid by the legal system to the unique character of what has become henceforth known as the *shoah*. It is undeniable that the Nazis' killing of the Jews remains a massacre without equivalent in history, for never before or since "has a state decided and announced under the authority of its supreme leader that a certain group of people had to be totally exterminated, to every extent possible — old people, women, and infants included — a decision that nation then put into practice with all the means at its disposal."[4] Given that the Jews are a diasporic people, that is, dispersed across the entire surface of the globe, the Nazi project had, moreover, a planetary dimension. It could not have been completely accomplished; the only ones affected, if one dares say such a thing, were European Jews. But, as Saul Friedlander has written,

> From the moment that a regime decides, basing itself on whatever criteria, that certain groups must be entirely annihilated and that they *are never again allowed to live on the earth*, a fundamental step has been taken. And I think that in modern history, this limit has only been crossed once — by the Nazis.[5]

11

It was, furthermore, this uniqueness, this incommensurability, this absolute singularity that led the international community to override its political realism and forge a new definition. It is precisely because the pretension "to decide who may and may not live upon this planet,"[6] because the legality of the massacre and the industrial treatment of the victims surpassed all bounds, defied all known norms, that the reference to the laws of humanity — up to that time purely Platonic — took on a resolutely binding character. By this fundamental gesture, civilization refused to go on accommodating itself to the violation of these laws by attributing such violations to either the unimpeachable sovereignty of the state or to the inevitable horrors of war. In the days following victory, the feeling prevailed that one could no longer, on pain of spiritual death, shrug off attacks on humanity as the mere gains and losses of international life.

But to find it legitimate, a half-century later, that the Nazis still monopolize the incrimination that grew out of their atrocities, and to say, like some, that having been a unique event, the destruction of the European Jews represents the one and only crime ever perpetrated against humanity — this is a gross misinterpretation. It is to confuse the encoding of laws of humanity in the legal system with the appearance of crimes against humanity in history; it is to interpret as a sign of vigilance the obvious failure of international society to institute a universal community through the creation of a repressive jurisdiction before which criminals of the state would have to answer for their acts. It is, in all good faith, to see the betrayed hope of Nuremberg as a promise kept; it is to give to cynicism or frailty the aura of remembrance and scruple; it is to mistake a law without teeth for an intransigent justice, an avowal of weakness for a position of principle, and an outburst from humanity for a triumph of the collective conscience. It is, in short, to convert the collapse

12

of civilization taking place before our eyes into a consecration of the *shoah*.

This quid pro quo, however, can be excused; this paralogical argument has attenuating circumstances. We would be less panicky and fearful of *banalization* and we could better defend the centrality of Auschwitz if we were not continually put on the defensive by all the speeches that, under the pretext of denouncing current atrocities or of establishing for members of the Resistance their rights as victims, undo the fundamental distinctions outlined at Nuremberg. In this we are less threatened by the danger of forgetting than by confusion or verbal intemperance — that is, the immoderate use of the words *Nazi* and *genocide* in indiscriminate contexts. If I had to summarize the Barbie trial in a single sentence, I would say that it provided an arena for converging and persistent maneuvers to pit a false victory on the part of memory against a meretricious broadening of the crime against humanity.

CHAPTER FOUR

HERO AND VICTIM

It was at Trzebinia, a small Polish village between Kracow and Katowice, that Primo Levi, newly released from Auschwitz by the Soviet army, first had a chance to communicate the experience that he had just lived through:

> Perhaps I was among the first dressed in "zebra" clothes to appear in that place called Trzebinia; I immediately found myself the centre of a dense group of curious people, who interrogated me volubly in Polish. I replied as best I could in German; and in the middle of the group of workers and peasants a bourgeois appeared, with a felt hat, glasses and a leather briefcase in his hand — a lawyer.
>
> He was Polish, he spoke French and German well, he was an extremely courteous and benevolent person; in short, he possessed all the requisites enabling me finally, after the long year of slavery and silence, to recognize in him the messenger, the spokesman of the civilized world, the first that I had met.
>
> I had a torrent of urgent things to tell the civilized world: my things, but everyone's, things of blood, things which (it seemed to me) ought to shake every conscience to its very foundations. In truth, the lawyer was courteous and benevolent: he questioned me, and I spoke at dizzy speed of those so recent experiences of mine, of Auschwitz nearby, yet, it seemed, unknown to all, of the hecatomb from which I alone had escaped, of every-

15

thing. The lawyer translated into Polish for the public. Now, I do not know Polish, but I know how one says "Jew" and how one says "political"; and I soon realized that the translation of my account, although sympathetic, was not faithful to it. The lawyer described me to the public not as an Italian Jew, but as an Italian political prisoner.

I had dreamed, we had always dreamed, of something like this, in the nights at Auschwitz: of speaking and not being listened to, of finding liberty and remaining alone. After a while I remained alone with the lawyer; a few minutes later he also left me, urbanely excusing himself.[1]

One must not imagine that such a fate of nonreception was unique to Poland. In France too, those known as the "racially deported" (to distinguish them from voluntary Resistance fighters) were received with a certain discomfort. Present in the very first parades following the Liberation, the "men in zebra clothes," as Primo Levi called them, disappeared very quickly from official commemorations. Not a single Jewish victim from the world of the Nazi concentration camps was among the fifteen mortal remains symbolically reunited around the flame of the Unknown Soldier on November 11, 1945. The government chose, quite naturally, two Resistance fighters from the country (a man and a woman), two deportees for acts of resistance (also a man and a woman), a prisoner killed in an attempted escape, and finally, nine military personnel from different branches and theaters of operation.[2] And it was not until 1954 that a national day was declared to commemorate the Deportation.

To be sure, France, unlike Poland, was not prey to persistent anti-Semitism; but it lived for the hour of the heroes and not for that of the victims. The collective consciousness was too busy rebuilding its virtue and — with the fiction of a people unanimously opposing the enemy — blotting out the less-than-glorious reality of the Occupation, to attend to the specificity of genocide. There was thus a discrepancy between the spirit of Nuremberg and public opinion. The Allies, who since 1941 had made the punishment of Nazi leaders one of their prime objectives, were forced almost in spite of themselves, under the shock of the horrors documented throughout the entire conflict, to distinguish another category of atrocities — unlinked to battle — from war crimes per se, crimes that were not effected against partisans or enemy armies and that were originally called "crimes of occupation," "crimes against public international order," and finally, "crimes against humanity." But France rebuilt its national identity around the Gaullist epic of underground soldiers fallen for their country, that is to say, in judicial terms, by supplanting crimes against humanity with war crimes.

The Resistance fighters themselves, rightly proud of having taken up arms against the occupiers, did not want to be confused with those whose identity, not actions, had taken them to Auschwitz or Buchenwald. On their return from the camps, most of them sought to emphasize that they had paid the price of action, not of "belonging." Deportation had not befallen them as a fate, but as a reprisal for their anti-German activities. They had deserved it, in a sense, and could even take pride in the fact that it was not the Nazis who decided their destiny — they themselves had knowingly exposed themselves to the risk of imprisonment, torture, and death. An implicit hierarchy of horror thus contrasted the individually risked death to the collectively administered death, the ordeal met head-on to the sentence accepted, and the courage of some to the passive suffering of others. In 1964, when the young Jewish writer J. F. Steiner wrote a book on the revolt that broke out in August 1943 at Treblinka — written, as he put it, to exorcise "the shame of

17

being one of the sons of this people of whom, at final count, six million members let themselves be led like sheep to the slaughter" — he received the Resistance's grand prize, in spite of the pain and indignation such statements aroused in the Jewish community.[3]

Thus if there was a silence about the "racially deported" in the years following the war, it was not because they were unable to speak (as a melodramatic and untrue cliché would have us believe) but because no one wanted to hear them. Beware of the pathos of the ineffable! The survivors of the Final Solution were not reduced to aphasia by a nameless misfortune, by an experience that no words could express; they had, on the contrary, an irrepressible need to bear witness, if only thereby to pay their debt to those who had perished. What was missing was an audience. "No sooner did we begin to tell our story," said Simone Veil recently, with undiminished anger, "than we were interrupted, like overexcited or overly talkative children, by parents who are themselves burdened down with real problems."[4]

We are no longer at that point; historians have irremediably blurred the edifying and mythic image of a partisan people, and "at the same time that the Resistance fighters were becoming forgotten, their ranks thinning with the years,"[5] the Jewish community learned to see in the genocide attempted against it a fundamental element of its identity. An ancient aristocratic principle — that persists in our society today — would have us believe that the glory of a man is reflected in his descendants. But even if the children of the Resistance fighters, legitimately proud of the commitment of their fathers, work hard to perpetuate their memory, they themselves are not Resistance fighters, whereas the children of the Jews, on the other hand, are Jewish. This existential difference (which is in no way a superiority), in time, could not help but influence collective awareness.

For all of these reasons, the prestige of the fighters no longer eclipses the disaster of the innocent victims; the commemoration of the Resistance has ceased to overshadow or to play down the memory of the Extermination. The embarrassment, the impatience or the condescension that greeted the first accounts of Simone Veil or of Primo Levi have given way to receptiveness and emotion. It can even be said that with *Shoah*, the film by Claude Lanzmann, the victims were admitted into the national consciousness on the same grounds and with the same rank as the heroes.

But, for all that, the competition of memories is not over yet. It was in fact reactivated by the Barbie trial. Recall that in the beginning, the magistrate in charge of investigating the dossier, Mr. Christian Riss, only retained the crimes against the Jews, and pronounced there to be no grounds for prosecution of the actions against the Resistance fighters. The latter, in his opinion, constituted war crimes, lapsed according to the statute of limitations since 1964 in France. The grand jury in Lyons at first confirmed this opinion, but when certain Resistance organizations came forward claiming damages the criminal court of appeals opted, on December 20, 1985, for an interpretation of crimes against humanity that was less restrictive or, to use the expression of the deputy director of public prosecution, Mr. Henri Dontenwille, less "thin-skinned" (*frileux*). Thereafter, included in this penal category were "inhuman acts and persecutions that, in the name of a state practicing a politics of ideological hegemony, have been committed in a systematic way not only against people by reason of their belonging to a racial or religious group but also against the opponents of this political system, whatever the form of their opposition."

19

Legally speaking, this ruling was no more nor less well-founded than that of the grand jury of Lyons. For reasons that will be analyzed later on, no clear doctrine can, in fact, be drawn from the charter signed in London to assure "the pursuit and punishment of the major criminals of the Axis Powers." While it solemnly enumerates the three great offenses brought to trial at Nuremberg, this text does not draw a clear and definitive line between war crimes and crimes against humanity.[6]

Given the circumstances, the decision of the supreme justices was welcome. By designating the abominable treatment of the Resistance fighters a crime against humanity, the Supreme Court of Appeals rightly avoided forcing a French lower court of assizes to judge — on the very site of his misdeeds — the man known as the "Butcher of Lyons," without being able to even mention the acts that earned him his name and his place in the national memory. And since the deportation of six hundred and fifty people on August 11, 1944 (that is, three weeks before the Liberation) figured among the charges retained against Barbie, the court was thus providentially spared having to morbidly sift out those whose deportation was a lapsed crime from those whose deportation was still punishable.

There was, nonetheless, something paradoxical in the spectacle of Resistance groups demanding an extension of crimes against humanity and asserting their right today to a status they had rejected in the past. "We the victims have never asked to be considered as heroes," Simone Veil has said, "so why do the heroes now want, at all costs and at the risk of mixing everything up, to be treated as victims?" Could it be because the symbolic ranking of war crimes and crimes against humanity has been surreptitiously inverted, ever since it was established that the latter alone have no statute of limitation?

There remains also the fact that any attempt to base an argument on the diplomatic fuzziness of the London Charter does not really do justice to the thinking that brought about the Nuremberg Trials — thinking reflected in the French bill of indictment:

> At different eras the world has seen bloody repressions directed against "enemies." We have also seen acts of gratuitous violence committed by ruffians and brutes acting on their own deranged instincts. But never before have we seen or could we have seen the scientific preparation of a massacre that was totally useless and unprovoked.[7]

In spite of the judges' decision, several speakers came forward during the trial to support this "restrictive" or "thin-skinned" point of view. First was André Frossard, who attempted throughout his deposition (and later in a small, luminous book)[8] to refute the ruling of the Court of Appeals by pointing out that there are no former fighters from Izieu, and by establishing, with an anecdote, the irreducible specificity of crimes against humanity:

> There was a Jew there, a good man, but whom an S.S. subaltern mistook for a Turk, because of his features. And one fine day this subaltern decided to make him recite in German this sentence: "A Jew is a parasite; he lives on the skin of the Aryan race." The poor man, not knowing German, couldn't do it, and at every mistake he was struck with punches and kicks. Finally he was able to learn the sentence, and thereafter, whenever he heard his torturer open the door, he would recite it on his own. And the day that he was called to be shot, the S.S. again made him recite the horrible sentence. That was it. A single grievance was enough: to be born Jewish.[9]

Then came Mrs. Alice Vansteenberghe, disabled since her "interrogation" by Barbie: "That morning, I had left my home

21

in the full euphoria of my living body; I never regained that feeling; I have never been able to walk again." Throwing the Resistance groups off-balance, she declared:

> We in the Resistance knew the risks we were taking, and I ac-
> cept everything that I suffered. But in the cell where I was
> thrown there were other people. I saw a Jewish woman and her
> child, well-groomed, very blonde, with a barrette in her hair.
> Well, one day Barbie walked in and came to take this mother
> from her child. This is not warfare — it's something unspeak-
> able, beyond all bounds.[10]

In fact, there is *the world* (*le monde*), of which war is still a part,
and there is the unspeakable, *beyond all bounds* (*l'immonde*). It is
not the same thing, to be an enemy and to be a hunted quarry. In
the first case, the world is still a world, for one is still the master
of one's choices. Even in the absence of freedom one is still free
to give or not give meaning to one's life — be it political meaning, by commitment, or ethical meaning, by the giving of one's
self, or epic meaning, by risking one's life. Even when one is
exposed to exceptional circumstances, even when stripped of
all rights, deprived of all basic guarantees, one can attest to
one's humanity through action. René Char wrote in 1944 in
Feuilles d'Hypnos:

> If I survive, I know that I will have to make a clean break from
> the atmosphere of these essential years, not to repress but to si-
> lently throw my "treasure" far away, to direct myself back to the
> humblest principles of conduct as in the days when I sought my-
> self without ever attaining valor.[11]

And on June 3, 1987, Mrs. Vansteenberghe confirmed this pre-
monition of nostalgia by evoking "the elite, of very exceptional
character, who had been brought together by the irregular

army of the Resistance," and the indestructible bonds that the common action had forged "between the humble mechanic and the university professor, the school teacher and the doctor."[12]

In the case of the victims, the years have no "atmosphere," for the world is no longer a world but a trap — one does not pay the penalty for one's acts, but for one's birth; one does not choose between survival or risk, tranquility or resistance — one is chosen and robbed of one's life before even deciding how to spend it. If one survives, the happiness of being alive becomes confused with that of reintegrating all the dimensions, all the prerogatives of the human condition — inauthenticity *and* authenticity, domestic tranquility and valor, the day-to-day routine of bourgeois life and the audacious freedom of activists.

This is why it will always be a mistake to contrast the heroism of the Jews who revolted against the destruction process to the law-abidingness of those who facilitated the Nazis' task by scrupulously carrying out their directives, as an attitude of resistance *vs.* an attitude of collaboration. Aside from the moral problem posed by the act of retrospectively (and comfortably) teaching the condemned the best way to die, the same words cannot be used indiscriminately for both war and genocide, except to reinsert "the world" (*le monde*) into what is "beyond all bounds" (*l'immonde*), and to make the no-exit situation of European Jews between 1939 and 1945 into a game.

Recall the last words of Klaus Barbie. Forcibly brought to the final hearing of his trial, he was asked at the end of the debates, according to custom, if he had anything to say. Since up until that moment he had chosen to be absent or silent, it was expected that he would decline this ritual invitation with a haughty "*Nichts zu sagen!*" But, departing for once from his own system of defense, he stood up and in impeccable French said, "I never committed the roundup in Izieu. I never had the power

23

to decide on deportations. I fought the Resistance, which I respect, with toughness, but that was war and the war is over."[13]

A declaration that was perhaps tactical and no doubt false. But it is not Barbie's sincerity that is the point here — it is the fact of seeing him, this unrepentant Nazi, reestablish a penal and ontological distinction that the court, with the best of intentions, had suppressed.

In this strange trial it was the Resistance fighters and not the official representatives of the Resistance, the accused and not the court who offered a rigorous definition of crimes against humanity.

CHAPTER FIVE

White Prisoners,
White
Executioners

A few dissenting voices thus reopened in court the debate the lawyers had wanted to close before the beginning of the trial. But to what avail? Of what use, what impact could these testimonies and the contradictions they brought to the official version of crimes against humanity be, since material humanity — flesh-and-blood humanity — let the judges and the prosecution down, undermined those who spoke in its name, and even carried sarcasm to the point of ostensibly choosing its designated assassins against its own spokesmen? If what Durkheim wrote is true — that "an act is criminal when it offends strong and definite states of the collective consciousness" — the presence on the bench of Jacques Vergès, Nabil Bouaïta, and Jean-Martin M'Bemba for the defense said in itself that the extermination of the Jews was a crime of local interest, a drop of European blood in the ocean of human suffering, and thus offended only the consciousness of white people.

Try to imagine for a moment at Nuremberg the Nazis' lawyers pleading the case of their clients (among others, Goering,

25

Bormann, Frank, Rosenberg, Kaltenbrunner, Julius Streicher) by quoting from André Gide's *Voyage to the Congo* and by passionately invoking their own experience of racism or of European colonialism. Such a grotesque scene is unimaginable. It took place forty years later, however, and without making too many waves, in the Palais de Justice at Lyons. The Barbie trial was therefore not, as most commentators claimed, an exemplary continuation of the Nuremberg Trials. Through the spectacular collusion of the representatives of the Third World with a Nazi torturer, it was, on the contrary, a mockery of the Nuremberg Trials, and it nullified the official finding established by the international community following the victory over the Nazis — that humanity *itself* is mortal.

Before Hitler, confidence reigned; no one believed that humanity could die. Of course, said the current metaphysics, individuals die — alone or en masse, violently or naturally, from disease or accident — but the human race renews itself, like other living species: "In every era, plants grow green and flower, insects hum, animals and men subsist in their indestructible youth, and every summer we rediscover the cherries already tasted a thousand times."[1] Moreover, human history advances. Men were aware of their finiteness, they knew themselves to be mortal; they also knew, from the beginning, that life never stopped. And since with the advent of the modern era they had reversed their relationship to the ancients — no longer considering them as patriarchs but as children "truly new in all things"[2] — they thought that humanity had broken away from its eternal rebirth, in order to grow from century to century and thereby to arrive, according to a dialectical or rectilinear trajectory, at a total mastery of its own destiny.

In a sense, death had its own double standard. It severed without pity individual lives ("The last act is bloody, no matter

how good the show is up until then — in the end they cover your
head with dirt and that's it"),[3] but it spared humanity. ("The
long procession of men over the course of the centuries must be
considered as one same man who always survives and continues
to learn.")[4] Thus everyone died, and nothing died. Everyone —
a people, a person — left a heritage that others coming after-
wards gathered up and brought to fruition. The wisdom of dead
civilizations was carried over into those that superseded them;
if man succumbed at the individual level, at the group level he
made continual progress. Fleeting and perishable, he simultaneously belonged to a forward-moving totality, perfectible and
immortal. His humanity, in the sense of human nature (as opposed to divine nature), or in the sense of the humane virtue of
gentleness (as opposed to inhumanity) was absorbed by humanity, in the sense of a generic and universal being. His acts,
his undertakings, his inventions — despite what he might do —
contributed to the collective product. His separate individu-
ality was taken in hand by a transcendental and unifying subject, a kind of all-encompassing "ego" whose Promethean
march ardently spanned the generations.

Within this evolutionary or revolutionary perspective, people's rights could very well be flouted here and there; such de-
plorable infringements never called into question the positive
movement of civilization. Even if, legally and morally, humanity
happened to come unhinged, historically it never ceased to
move forward, to progress in the accomplishment of its
vocation — to pursue, with indefatigable energy, its march toward exhaustive knowledge and betterment. An event that,
from the point of view of sensibility, was an unjustifiable scandal, appeared — as soon as one took the point of view of
evolution — as a minor accident, if not a ploy, of the reason un-
derlying the order of things. Beneath the appalling guises of vi-

27

olence or barbarity, human passions conveyed the destiny of superior ends, and attested to the role played by human
unsociability within the very career of humanity. "It's not true
that a straight line is always the shortest distance," Lessing had
warned in *The Education of the Human Race*. In other words, history progressed also by its bad side, and it contradicted the universal conditions defining humanity only in order to subse-
quently give birth to a humanity truly and universally humane.
The triumphal procession of history thus marched over those
bodies strewn on the ground;[5] the blood (*le sang*) of the victims
was drained into the meaning (*le sens*) of the future; individual
tragedies were compensated by the universal epic; as they say
in French, broken eggs make a fine omelette. In short, the idea
of humanity remained untouched by harsh realities and was a
more efficient consolation for evil than all the ancient the-
odicies.

At Nuremberg, this consolation stopped working. Historical
realism was denounced there along with political realism. If the
floor was given over to the lawyers and magistrates, it is because
it was no more possible to "write off the death camps as work-
related accidents in the victorious advancement of civilization,"[6] than it was to resign oneself to the fact that the relations
between countries are governed by force and not by law. Furthermore, how was it possible to persist in converting suffering
into reason, to forget the men who die in favor of the Man who
marches forward, when it was this forward march that had
made possible this industrialized death? There is nothing more
regimented, more methodical, more modern than the Final Solution. This "criminal enterprise against the human condition"[7]
did not burst forth from the depths of time to convulsively undo
the patient work of civilization. In this unleashing of a cruelty
without limits, progress was implicated in its technological

form (the sophistication of the death machine) as well as in its moral form (domestication of urges, submission of will to the law).

In the aftermath of the First World War, Valéry wrote:

> We have seen, seen with our own eyes conscientious work, the most solid teaching, the most serious discipline and assiduity adapted to unspeakable projects. . . . So many horrors would not have been possible without so many virtues. A lot of science was needed, no doubt, in order to kill so many people, to waste so many assets, to obliterate so many cities in such a short time — but moral qualities were no less needed. Knowledge and Duty, are you then suspect?[8]

In 1945, this suspicion became a certainty. Life had surely resumed its busy course, but *its victims could no longer be chalked up to progress*, and history ceased to be that cartoon in which the hero — battered, mutilated, robbed of speech, crushed — always rises up again intact (if not strengthened) to continue his throbbing adventure. It was clear that this time the blow was mortal. From whatever angle one looked at it, *the crime was murder*. The human race had been forever impoverished by the destruction of the world of European Jews. A catastrophe had taken place that no logic could possibly efface; no amount of reason could attenuate its irrevocable nature. That is why, instead of letting mankind continue on its way without dwelling on the wounds inflicted on individuals, men themselves decided to dwell at length on the wound that Nazism had inflicted on humanity.[9]

And the dogma of humanity's self-fulfilling destiny through history was refuted not only by the scope and meticulousness of the crime; it was also compromised by the statements of the torturers. As Jankélévitch has rightly noted, the extermination of

29

the Jews "was doctrinally founded, philosophically explained, methodically prepared by the most pedantic doctrinarians ever to have existed."[10] The Nazis were not, in effect, brutes, but theorists. It was not because of blood-thirsty instincts, economic or political interests, or even because of prejudice that they sacrificed all scruples. On the contrary, it could be said that the objections and scruples of interest, of instinctive pity, and of prejudice were sacrificed on the altar of their philosophy of history. "It is thus an erroneous and stupid conception," Theodore Fritsch commented as early as 1910 in his *Anti-Semite's Catechism*, "to explain the opposition to Judaism as an outgrowth of a stupid racial and religious hatred, whereas in fact it is a disinterested battle animated by the most noble ideals, against an enemy of humanity, morality and culture."[11] As faithful disciples of this benevolent anti-Semitism, the Nazis felt that they were accomplishing a spiritual mission by taking what Himmler called "the grave decision to make the Jewish people disappear from the face of the earth," and in refusing, up to the end, to be deterred from this objective, even by the efforts of war. In the service of mankind, these metaphysical killers broke all the bonds of humanity, from morality to calculated self-interest.

Here is Primo Levi's account:

> Panwitz is tall, thin, blond; he has eyes, hair, and nose as all Germans ought to have them, and sits formidably behind a complicated writing-table. I, Häftling 174517, stand in his office, which is a real office, shining, clean and ordered, and I feel that I would leave a dirty stain on whatever I touched.
>
> When he finished writing, he raised his eyes and looked at me.
>
> From that day I have thought about Doktor Panwitz many times and in many ways. I have asked myself how he really functioned as a man; how he filled his time, outside of the Polymer-

30

ization and the Indo-Germanic conscience; above all when I was once more a free man, I wanted to meet him again, not from a spirit of revenge, but merely from a personal curiosity about the human soul.

Because that look was not one between two men; and if I had known how completely to explain the nature of that look, which came as if across the glass window of an aquarium between two beings who live in different worlds, I would also have explained the essence of the great insanity of the third Germany.[12]

Impossible, after such an experience, to continue to believe in the grandeur of a collective destiny that contains and surpasses the existence of individuals. For what gives Doctor Panwitz's gaze its coldness (without pity but also without hate) is the absolute certainty of contributing, through the elimination of parasites, to the accomplishment of the human race.

Thus civilization discovered (or rediscovered) in 1945 that men are not the *means*, the instruments, or the representatives of a superior subject — humanity — that is fulfilled through them, but that humanity is their responsibility, that they are its *guardians*. Since this responsibility is revocable, since this tie can be broken, humanity found itself suddenly stripped of the divine privilege that had been conferred on it by the various theories of progress. Exposed and vulnerable, humanity itself can die. It is at the mercy of men, and most especially of those who consider themselves as its emissaries or as the executors of its great designs. The notion of crimes against humanity is the legal evidence of this realization.

Speaking as delegates of nonwhite humanity and displaying their colors like banners, the three lawyers for Klaus Barbie (the Congolese M'Bemba, the Algerian Bouaïta, and the French-Vietnamese Vergès) wanted to wipe out the lesson of

Nuremberg. They could have sought attenuating circumstances for their client, could have emphasized the difference in
the scope of the atrocities committed by the Nazis and the mar-
ginal role of the head of the Lyons Gestapo in the extermination
process. They could have portrayed Barbie as a formidable police officer, exclusively charged with dismantling the Resistance. They could thereby have used the crimes whose statute of limitations had expired, and of which he was in fact
guilty, to counter the crimes without limitations for which he
was arraigned. They could have, finally, invoked the bureau-
cratic excuse of obedience to orders, the sociological excuse of
indoctrination, and the psychological excuse of a difficult
coming-of-age in a ravaged Germany. Without completely dis-
daining this classical argument, they preferred to set themselves up as accusers, and to transfer the racism of the crime
itself onto the memory of the crime. Or, one might say, to transfer the racism of the crime from Doctor Panwitz — whose gaze
upon Primo Levi clearly said, "This something in front of me
belongs to a species which it is obviously opportune to sup-
press. In this particular case, one has to first make sure that it
does not contain some utilizable element"[13] — onto all those
who today persist in honoring the victims of that madness, or
who bring to trial the surviving agents of that madness.

"You ask us to suffer with you, but your memories are not
ours, and your narcissistic lamentations do not bring tears to
our eyes," was the message to the Western world from Mr.
Vergès and his satellites. They said, in effect, "It is you who refuse to share the earth with other races; it is you who, mistaking
yourself for the center of the universe, seek to fill with your single existence, with your single race, the concept of humanity
and the archives of history. It is you who, not content with having the wealth and the power, demand in addition, sympathy —

and who try to make yourselves pitied by the very people whom you continue to exploit, after years of treating them as subhuman. Whites, you have pity for the fate of whites. Europeans, you inflate a family quarrel into a world war and crime without limitation. As infatuated with yourselves as you are indifferent to the sufferings of the truly oppressed, you only attend to your own scrapes and bruises, and you elevate the Jews — that is, your own — to the dignity of a condemned race or of chosen martyrs, in order to make people forget, by your one-time ordeal, the cruelties that you have never ceased to inflict upon the races of the south. But point your finger as you may at Barbie and his ilk for the world's condemnation; go ahead and drench the Nazi crimes with your long, tearful sobs — echoed and amplified by the huge force of the media at your disposal; we are there, face-to-face with you in this place, and our multicolored presence proves that, in spite of all your efforts, the manipulation has failed. Through our intervention, in fact, it is humanity itself that bursts out laughing, and which says that *your* disaster is not *its* business."

What is striking in such reasoning is not the fact of men acting as devil's advocates, using all of their talents' resources to render Barbie innocent of the horrible acts he was accused of (this mission was imperatively conferred upon them by state law, which would repudiate itself if it withdrew its guarantees to certain categories of criminals); rather, it is striking to see resurfacing, on the occasion of the trial of an SS officer, a tradition that might not have been expected to survive the attempted extermination of the Jews by the Nazis: left-wing anti-Dreyfusism.

In the same way the most rigid spokesmen of the proletariat refused to take Dreyfus's part because they did not want to be side-tracked from the revolutionary struggle by a fratricidal

33

battle between two rival factions of the *bourgeoisie*, similarly, for Messrs. Vergès, M'Bemba, and Bouaïta the six million Jews killed under Hitler had no right to universal commiseration, since in the Final Solution it was white prisoners and white executioners; when a massacre took place in the camp of the enemies of Man, one could not ask the other camp — that is, those in charge of humanity's progress — to sink into eternal mourning.

These militant lawyers were thus not content to merely plead their client's case as best they could — by treating the *victims* of Hitler's racism as *symptoms* of Western racism and imperialism, they reintroduced the metaphysics shattered by the catastrophe in its most radical version; they recast humanity once again as a "forward-moving totality," and made men themselves the instruments or adversaries of its achievement.

It is true that Soviet propaganda had for a long time paved the way for them. Stalinist Russia, present at Nuremberg, had easily adopted the penal category of "crimes against humanity" but without abandoning its Promethean faith in the march of history. Far from seeing Auschwitz as a refutation of progress, they saw Hitler as the paradigm and the paroxysm of all the reactionary forces allied against progress. Protean enemy, thousand-headed hydra, the Führer had been destroyed only to immediately reappear in other places and under other guises. As Ilya Ehrenbourg wrote in the volume of his memoirs entitled *Russia at War*, "What is called into question here, is the fact that of the fifty million victims of World War II, there is one missing: Fascism. It survived 1945. To be sure, it had a period of *malaise* and decline, but it did not die."[14] A handy principle, which until recently allowed the Soviet government to "Nazify" all adversaries that came along, from unempowered dissidents to American nuclear might.

But this propaganda, which is today (for the time being?) more moderate, retained through the power of things a memory link with the event from which it had sprung. The same can no longer be said (as the Barbie trial demonstrated) about the religious or secular ideologies now competing with Soviet Communism for humanity's torch. Nor can it be said of history's new subjects, who, outside the West, want to take up where the European proletariat or socialist homeland left off. Frenchmen at Sétif, Americans at My Lai, Jews of the UGIF (Union Générale des Israélites de France, created by the Vichy regime in 1941 as a replacement for all existing Jewish organizations), or Zionists at Deir Yassin — everyone, in effect, according to Mr. Vergès, is a Nazi, everyone except the Nazis themselves. Because they are the losers. Crushed by the Allies, having served as a guarantee or an excuse for the creation and expansion of the racist State of Israel, how could they be totally bad — that is, Nazi? Faced with two aspects of the West, with two modalities of horror, it was thus choosing the lesser of two evils to defend one who had been *vanquished*. And furthermore, at the very moment when the offspring of the deportees were — in good conscience — hounding Palestinians in Libya or the West Bank, didn't Klaus Barbie shake his black lawyer's two hands without the slightest hint of racist hesitation, as the lawyer movingly revealed to us during his closing speech for the defense?[15]

At Nuremberg, the world judged history, instead of submitting to its verdicts or seeking the truth in its unfolding. Defining the human race by its *diversity* and no longer by its *forward march*, realizing that it is not Man who inhabits the earth, but men in their infinite plurality,[16] the judges spoke in the name of all of international society, because, as they thought, it was society as a whole that had suffered an irreparable wrong "by the fact of the disappearance of one of its racial, national, or cultural elements."[17]

This new perception of humanity no doubt accelerated the struggle against racial segregation in the United States and contributed to the downfall of colonialism in Europe. It was under the effects of the Nazis' shocking destruction of the Jews that the movement for the integration of American blacks received its momentum[18] and public opinion in the West was able to consider and oppose as *attacks on humanity* the violations committed by its own imperialism — from the former slave trade to the contemporary wars in Algeria and Vietnam. As Paul Ricoeur writes, profoundly, "The victims of Auschwitz are, par excellence, delegates to our memory for all the victims of history."[19]

Now, in Lyons in 1987, in the first trial conducted in France for crimes against humanity, the defense lined up the martyrs of colonialism and the black slave trade in the camp of the accused; it did this by reducing the diversity of the human race to the history of Man, and by pitting this Man (for whom it claimed to be the only true representative in the courtroom) against the Nazism of white-Jewish Europe.

Sheer delirium? Except for two former leaders of the Algerian National Liberation Front,[20] no one withdrew their symbolic mandate from this defense that boasted "all the colors of the human rainbow";[21] no intellectual, no poet, no journalist, no African, Asian, or Arab leader spoke up to say that one could neither accuse Jewish pain of obstructing the world's memory nor present former slaves or former victims of colonialism as victims of "the conspiracy of the remnants of Zion."

This tacit (and sometimes noisy)[22] approval suggests that if France had decided to present its prisoner to the United Nations, in keeping with the wish expressed by Hannah Arendt at the time of the Eichmann trial, numerous countries would have followed Vergès and voted for an acquittal. For a large segment of international opinion, Hitler has nothing to do with Hitler, nor does the Third Reich have anything to do with the catastrophe of humanity. For this majority inhabiting the planet, what remains from World War II is a word: Nazi. A word henceforth without referent, anchored to nothing, a word that is no longer a fact but simply a label, a floating word — available, completely adaptable — that regroups under one infamous heading every form of opposition the self-proclaimed representatives of forward-marching Man encounter in their path. A word, to put it differently, that denies the adversary the very quality of being human, degrades him into a monster against whom all means are justified, and, failing that, can consecrate as anti-Nazism the two practices that were judged and solemnly condemned at Nuremberg: total war and extermination.

CHAPTER SIX

THE INCIDENT

The defense, a priori, was not content to stop there. It had announced two counterproceedings: against the West, and against the Resistance. "Jean Moulin will be present at the hearing, if it comes to that, for such is my decision," Mr. Vergès had warned, with his usual arrogance. To be sure, the court had disallowed the use of the Caluire affair by the prosecution, but Barbie's lawyer seemed convinced that without the arrest and death of Jean Moulin, the name of Klaus Barbie would have disappeared from national memory, and that the former SS officer could, like many of his colleagues, have continued to live out his days quietly somewhere in South America. Even if today other infamies were being brought forward against him, it was that crime above all which had snatched him from anonymity and had inscribed him in the French collective consciousness. By affirming — indeed by having the accused himself affirm — that Jean Moulin did not die under torture but that he had fractured his skull against a wall after realizing that he had been denounced by his comrades in arms, Mr. Vergès hoped to prove that the Resistance (human, all too human) was in part responsible for that event which had given the Lyons Gestapo chief his cumbersome notoriety. Against the black-and-white setting of the legend, he wanted to oppose "the bitter truth" of a night when all soldiers were gray—the soldiers of the underground as well as soldiers of the Occupation. In short, he wanted to demonstrate that there were no saints or sinners, none completely guilty or completely just, and that the "Butcher of Lyons" was the scapegoat of our mythology, the villain we needed to isolate degradation—to exorcise, via a reassuring Manichaeism, the evil that was everywhere.

Opting for the "effect" of an announcement rather than for a surprise effect, Mr. Vergès developed and honed this argument over the four years that passed between the capture of Barbie and his trial. In a book that appeared in November 1983, he imputes to the pro-Jewish stance of Robert Badinter (then minister of justice) the fact that his client was no longer answerable for the death of Jean Moulin: "The legal argument that the floor—that is, the power that it is hierarchically subject to—advances to explain this evasion is that the arrest and deportation of a Jew is a crime against humanity, but that the arrest and death of Jean Moulin should be a war crime, and that war crimes have expired, according to the statute of limitations."[1] Which clearly means that between two equal persecutions, the lord chancellor shamelessly favors the one that strikes closest to home. But, warns Mr. Vergès, "I will show via undisputable and undisputed testimony the inexorable march of events toward the drama and then the passion of Jean Moulin, and I will leave out nothing that touches on the responsibilities of each person."[2] His scenario is the following: Jean Moulin was turned over to the Germans by members of the Resistance who found him both too Gaullist and to close to the Communists, and who had established, against his will, ties with the American secret service. When interviewed on French television that same month, Vergès affirmed he could demonstrate that if "Jean Moulin died, it was not from blows received at Barbie's hands; it was because, faced with the breadth of the betrayal around him, he considered it the only way he could behave with dignity."[3] An accusation he reiterated the following year in Claude Bal's film, *Que la vérité est amère* (The bitter truth).

Forewarned of the intentions and strategy of Mr. Vergès, the lawyers representing the plaintiffs from the Resistance thus had plenty of time to polish their response, and they were determined not to let the defense transform itself into the prosecution. But — surprise number 1 — the debates did not arouse any incident. Barbie chose to be absent, and Mr. Vergès was careful not to raise the question of Jean Moulin, even on the day when the bar summoned the members of the Resistance he had quoted, those he had promised to show were "heroes with feet of clay" — "people who lived a double life, people whose partisan political passion made them forget service to the Resistance."[4]

Was this curious discretion merely a ruse? Was Mr. Vergès forced to abandon such attacks by the judgment handed down in Paris on April 30, 1987 — only a few days before the beginning of the trial — that condemned Claude Bal for the defamation of the Resistance fighters who were implicated in his film? Or was Vergès reserving his punches for his closing speech — for that solemn and final moment when the adversary can no longer reply without violating the sacrosanct rights of the defense? Fearing this ultimate stratagem, Mr. Noguères warned his colleague that his final speech for the defense would not be inviolable, that he could not do whatever he wanted during it, and that bypassing custom, he himself would interrupt it in order to make any necessary revisions if Mr. Vergès began to reiterate his calumnious imputations about the members of the Resistance.[5]

Surprise number 2 — Mr. Vergès complied. He did not carry

41

out his threat. The promise of creating a scandal was not fulfilled. Despite the rendezvous Vergès himself announced, Jean Moulin did not figure in the interminable speech for the defense. Most observers saw this as a complete rout of the defense lawyer. All it had taken were some stern looks to make him show respect — he who throughout the proceedings had predicted that Barbie would be surreptitiously killed in his cell, rather than be allowed to publicly sully the image of the Resistance. The spell was thus broken; the *grand provocateur* was nothing but a blusterer, and Bernard-Henri Lévy could write triumphantly, on the eve of the verdict,

> We were afraid of Vergès, if you can believe it. We were afraid of provocations, of the revelations that he was going to make. The entire country was in suspense to hear the words, the names, that he was going to reveal. Today Vergès has lost. He hasn't kept a single one of his promises, he hasn't pulled off any of his special "effects." And he, who had such high expectations of this affair — who was counting on not just a triumph but the crowning of his career — he will probably leave behind no more of a trace than did the obscure Dr. Servatius of the Eichmann trial in Jerusalem.[6]

Frivolous optimism. For an incident burst out right in the middle of the closing speeches. And the defense was backed up spectacularly by the very people who, since the beginning of the trial, had kept it under surveillance. Let us recall that when the representative of the Federation of Jewish Societies in France, Mr. Zaoui, took it upon himself to interrupt the final speech for the defense by Mr. Bouaïta, Barbie's Algerian lawyer, who evoked, among other things, "the Nazification of Israeli Jews,"[7] all of the spokesmen of the Resistance protested this inappropriate behavior. Such an interruption, legitimate when made by Mr.

Noguères on behalf of the members of the Resistance, was deemed sacrilegious as soon as Mr. Zaoui used it on behalf of the Jews. How does one explain such a double standard? How could defamation be outlawed in one case and not in the other?

The reaction of Mr. La Phuong, lawyer for the Resistance association Ceux de la Libération (The Liberationists) sheds light on this question. By exclaiming, "I am not here as the defender of the State of Israel!" he indicated that Mr. Zaoui, himself, was, and that his gesture was motivated not by concern for the truth, but by self-interest and by the image of the country he was representing to the courtroom. Only a militant Zionist — and further, a hypersensitive one — could contest the defense's right to identify the Palestinian refugee camps of Sabra and Shatila with Auschwitz, phosphorous bombs with the crematoriums, and the Jewish notion of the "chosen people" with Hitler-style racism. Faced with this offended nationalism, Barbie's lawyers and the lawyers for the Resistance found themselves on the same side of the fence. They separately and severally led the same battle to dislodge the Jews from their position of uniqueness and to wrench crimes against humanity away from those who would monopolize them. Asked by the newspaper *Libération* to make a judicial assessment of the trial, Paul Bouchet, the former president of the bar of Lyons, went so far as to say,

> The presence beside Jacques Vergès of an Algerian lawyer and a Congolese lawyer has internationalized the defense. A purely domestic defense would no doubt have created less of a stir, but it would not perhaps have asked the questions so strongly — questions that, upsetting as they may be, are useful when it is a matter of defining, in a law that is still being formulated, the limits of crimes against humanity.[8]

43

For this eminent member of the legal profession who, before being named to the state council, was in charge of coordinating the various plaintiffs' lawyers, there was thus no scandal, no cause for amazement, for anger, or for questioning in the close alliance between the "master race" and the nonwhite humanity. On the contrary, Paul Bouchet commended the defense's contribution to the progress of conscience and to the perfecting of the law. According to him, Mr. Vergès's relentless insistence that Auschwitz was not the anus of the world but the navel of the West had provoked a violent shock, but, in the balance, a salutary one. These "disturbing" questions were necessary, he suggested, to pursue the legal deliberations initiated by the plaintiffs from the Resistance, and they would further allow our legal system to free itself finally from the "thin-skinned" ethnocentrism that had confined it since Nuremberg. Could Barbie's lawyer dream of a greater victory, a more brilliant ratification than this mark of universalism discerned in his actions?[9]

CHAPTER SEVEN

EMOTIONAL CONFUSION

"The interpretation of a text in the penal code should not be *cool* and *thin-skinned*, or, on the other hand, *feverish*," said Lyons's public prosecutor, Pierre Truche, soon after the Supreme Court of Appeals handed down the judgment that caused certain acts previously considered war crimes to be included in the definition of crimes against humanity. Going against popular opinion, this singular and obstinant magistrate refused to abandon legal deliberations on mass murder to the purely psychological (if not physiological) alternatives of hot and cold — tenderness or hardness of heart. To the assistant public prosecutor of criminal chambers — who had carried the decision by saying, "I, for one, know that the six hundred unfortunates of the convoy of August 11, 1944, heard the same raucous cry in the early hours of the morning: 'You are summoned, no baggage necessary' " — Truche even dared to reply (at the risk of damaging his case and of appearing positively glacial) that the Germans were the first to distinguish the fates of those various deportees, by disembarking the male Resistance workers at the Alsatian camp of Struthof, the female Resistance members at Ravensbruck, and the Jews — men, women, and children — at Birkenau, where they, and they alone, were destined for immediate death. The chances of survival not being the same, one

45

could argue that for the Nazi bureaucrats, each of these destinations corresponded to a different fate.

The choice of Pierre Truche to represent the prosecution in the trial was made, it seems, in the same spirit as his making, from the very beginning of the indictment, a special issue of the forty-four young boarders from the Jewish colony of Izieu — recalling that there were "greater degrees of horror, in horror," and that this greater degree of horror was "the genocide of children."[1]

Let us pause for a moment over this expression, "the genocide of children." While it is striking at first sight or at first hearing, when subjected to even the slightest scrutiny it becomes impossible and absurd. For genocide is the attempt to destroy a race, and the Nazis never attempted to annihilate the race of children. Their propaganda never denounced the conspiracy of children or the devastating effects of the "bacillus" of childhood. It was not children whom Hitler described as "garbage that pollutes," "a pack of rats," "an abscess" that must be immediately "lanced." Nor was it because they ranged in age from three to thirteen years that the inhabitants of the home at Izieu were rounded up on April 6, 1944, and sent to the death camps, but because they belonged to a parasitic race whose total liquidation had been programmed at the Conference of Wannsee.

One may object that I am criticizing a figure of speech as though it were a reasoned argument, and that the prosecutor substituted the part (the children) for the whole (the Jews) for rhetorical purposes, knowing full well what he meant. Wanting the courtroom to share his feelings, he spoke wrongly for the laudable purpose of touching rightly. In fact, there is nothing more immediately evocative, nothing that arouses in us such ardent compassion as the unleashing of brute strength against ab-

solute innocence or weakness. But therein lies the problem —
or, if you will — the redoubtable emotional impact of the expression "genocide of children." This metonymy makes the finality of the crime disappear behind its very inhumanity. It is
not the outrageous refusal to share the earth with another race
that it asks us to feel and ponder, but cruelty itself, the essence
of evil. Not the question of particular intentions, but barbarism,
plain and simple. Not the most systematic attack ever made on
the *human race*, but the most radical negation conceivable of *human goodness*.

And if the crime against humanity is defined simply as the
most inhuman, the most monstrous of all crimes, if it only is dis-
tinguished from other unlawful or immoral acts by the degradation that it reveals, all the arguments for keeping a cool head
and for maintaining surveillance over legal distinctions collapse; one would have to be not only "cool" but ferocious and
pitiless to continue to see in the persecution of Resistance members an acceptable act of barbarism or a *human crime*. And the
torture that takes place in military dictatorships? And "mis-
takes" made by the police? And the murder of old women or the
rape of children? According to this logic, which is that of the
heart, it is through lack of sensitivity, it is because humanity is
not humane enough, that there still exist ignoble acts falling
outside of the category of crimes against humanity. And the
broader the sphere covered by this offense becomes, the closer
humankind will come to that ideal state where, united against
crime, it can finally proclaim everything inhuman to be alien
to it.

By conjuring up the image of the genocide of children, the
unbearable evocation of Izieu led the prosecutor to the place
where neither competing memories nor the West's bad conscience had succeeded in bringing him, and he was thus able to

enlarge upon the high court's argument in the very name of the issue that had first provoked their difference of opinion — the policy of extermination:

> We did not agree. The magistrates of Lyons, in conformity with my indictments, had adopted Mr. Frossard's definition, which limits crimes against humanity to acts committed against the Jews. We had thought that the members of the Resistance, being voluntary combatants, were not involved. The Supreme Court of Appeals did not follow our lead. It considered the treatment inflicted in the Nazi camps to result in inhumanity. At this point I must tell you my conviction as a man and as a citizen. The Supreme Court having decided that everything that you have now heard recounted is inhuman, the debate, in my opinion, is nonetheless not closed. I profoundly hope that this trial does not mark the end of deliberations on the unacceptable. If there was something shocking in distinguishing among the deportees of the convoy of August 11, 1944, according to whether they were Jewish or members of the Resistance, differences still exist, since the Supreme Court of Appeals decreed that the charges of torturing Resistance members not be retained, while such torturing of Jews before their deportation constitute, for the responsible party, aggravating circumstances. Your decision will thus intervene to mark a stage. At present, I suggest that you consider all the facts that are submitted to you as crimes against humanity, *for you cannot say that there is a single act in this dossier that is not inhuman.*[2]

Denouncing the murder of children, extending the limits of the unacceptable — what man of good will could refuse to join forces with such noble ambition? Not Mr. Roland Dumas, who, charged with concluding for all the plaintiffs, succeeded in making the audience weep by presenting an inventory of the child martyrs of today. Nor did he hesitate to include in this

48

category the political militants who had been kidnapped, tortured, and executed by the Argentine junta — on the grounds that it was *their mothers* who had publicly called the executioners to account. He went on:

> In my country it is customary to bury a dead child in a white shroud, since white is the symbol of innocence, and every death of a child is a tragedy for humanity. This is the message that you must pass on — and well beyond our own borders. It must reach South Africa, where children are in prison and in danger, the Middle East, where they live in fear of bombs, Argentina, where the mothers of the May Square incident demanded in vain their own.[3]

Nor could Messrs. M'Bemba and Bouaïta refuse to partake in this denunciation of inhumanity, they who were ostensibly a part of the humanitarian crusade preached by the chief prosecutor; they thus enjoyed the luxury of putting their defense of Barbie under the moral authority of the prosecution. Nor, in the end, could Mr. Vergès, who, taking at his word the man he always designated in grandiloquent style and tone (now habitual with him) his "only adversary," went so far as to dedicate the published version of his closing speech for the defense to "children martyred in all wars: Jewish, Palestinian, Vietnamese, Algerian . . . and not forgetting the seventy German children who died from privation in the camp at Montreuil-Bellay and are buried in the military cemetery at Huisnes."[4] The sentimental dilution of crimes against humanity in "general inhumanity" thus justified putting white-Jewish Europe on trial, and brought the unhoped-for support of the *heart* to the alliances forged by the defense in the name of *Ideology.*   49

CHAPTER EIGHT

THE NIGHT

OF THE IDYLL

What is Ideology? According to Hannah Arendt, it is "the logic of an idea," the claim to explain history as "one consistent process"[1] whose conclusion is the accomplishment, the production of humanity itself. Ideology thus refuses all relevance to the distinction made at Nuremberg between massacres committed in the name of the law by a "criminal public service" and violations by certain countries, in certain circumstances, of their own internal law. For what Ideology calls law is the formal expression of evolution and nothing else. Whether it speaks of the "law of history" or the "law of life," whether it refers to Marx or Darwin, Ideology places humanity in submission to the same rule as nature — that is, to an order that is not a commandment. The ends that men propose for themselves and the imperatives they impose on themselves dissimulate, in the eyes of Ideology, the causes that make them act. In short, Ideology substitutes necessity for duty and the scientific law of "becoming" for the transcendence of judicial or moral law. While using legal terminology, it excludes the law from its vision of the world. In Ideology, Hannah Arendt describes how "the term *law* itself changed its meaning: from expressing the framework of stability within which human actions and motions can take place, it became the expression of the motion itself."[2]

For Mr. Vergès, the north/south conflict being the law of history, France in Algeria and the United States in Vietnam showed their true face as predators, torturers, antihumanitarians. And if it is true that internal public opinion against the war carried weight in these two countries, this did not spring from the contradiction between the *values* of the West and its *crimes* — it only means that the West at that moment revealed its criminal essence to a significant number of Westerners.

And in the same way that the truth about the West comes down to its imperialistic violence, so crimes committed by nonwestern nations do not exist by virtue of their positive evolutionary role. Armed with this line of argument, Barbie's lawyers achieved the marvel of relentlessly demanding the broadening of crimes against humanity by systematically pushing aside all the recognized cases of "criminal public service," and even by reintroducing in the courtroom the kind of logic that could lead to their emergence.

The extermination of three million Cambodians was not, in fact, the result of a passing fury or an outburst of bestiality. The youthful cadres of Angkar (this genocide was carried out by adolescents) had the same gaze as Doctor Panwitz; with an implacable calm they executed the sentence pronounced by history against those who carried the mark of Western influence, and they thus pushed Ideology to its ultimate consequences. It was in the name of the law that they overcame the moral imperative "Thou shalt not kill." It was the "science" in them, and not nature, that smothered the voice of conscience. It was *idea* that dominated *instinct*, and not, as in the pogroms, instinct that unleashed all its force. As Hannah Arendt has written, "Terror is the realization of the law of movement; its chief aim is to make it

52

possible for the force of nature or of history to race freely through mankind, unhindered by any spontaneous human action."[3]

Thus, in this trial, which became for the defense the trial of all genocides, and in which the deputy director of public prosecution himself descried a deepening of judicial thought, the Khmer Rouge revolution was scarcely considered. Analysis of that event, however, could not have failed to bring to light the true deficiencies of Nuremberg. With its methodical elimination of the bourgeoisie and the intelligentsia (recognizable by the fact that they wore glasses and spoke several languages) and of all the enemies of the New Man, the Pol Pot regime directly inscribed itself in the murderous lineage of the Hitler regime. Whereas formerly crimes took place "counter to a moral law, which was simultaneously in effect," in this case, as in the case of the Nazis, "it was the crime that was transformed into doctrine and moral law."[4] But since that crime was not perpetrated within the framework or advancement of a war, the judgment at Nuremberg does not allow for its punishment. In fact, after some hesitation, the allied military court finally decided to restrict the notion of the crime against humanity to those crimes committed *in time of war:*

> It is beyond all doubt, one reads in the judgment, that even before the war political opponents of Nazism were being killed or interned in concentration camps. The regime in these camps was odious. Terror often reigned — it was organized and systematic. A politics of harassment, repression, and murder was pursued without scruple toward civilians presumed hostile to the government; the persecution of Jews was already rampant. But in order to be considered crimes against humanity, acts of this sort committed before the war must be part of a plot or a concerted plan executed with the design of unleashing and further-

53

ing a war of aggression. They must at least be related to this. Now, the Tribunal does not find that the proof of this relationship has been established, however revolting and atrocious the acts in question may sometimes have been. It cannot therefore declare that these acts imputed to Nazism and taking place before September 1, 1939, constitute, in the sense of the statute, crimes against humanity.[5]

The judgment at Nuremberg was thus made in two stages: having clearly foreseen a distinct category of crimes, having affirmed — through the American delegate to the United Nations Judicial Committee on War Crimes — that "the crimes perpetrated against stateless persons or against any other people by reason of their race or religion must be considered crimes against humanity" because they attacked the very foundations of civilization, independent of their place or date, and independent of whether or not they constituted infractions of the laws and customs of war,[6] the Allies then limited, *in fine*, their legal jurisdiction to crimes committed *after* the outbreak of hostilities. They originally rejected the arguments of realism, as we have seen, only to rally around them in the end, sacrificing on the altar of noninterference the universal principles they had just affirmed. Fearful of endangering all international order, they engaged in a difficult compromise between reference to a law of all mankind and the idea that a government has the right to do at home what it does not have the right to do outside its borders. As the American justice Robert Jackson, responsible for preparing the case, explained at the Charter Conference in London:

54

It has been a general principle from time immemorial that the internal affairs of another government are not ordinarily our business; that is to say, the way Germany treats its inhabitants, or any other country treats its inhabitants, is not our affair any more than it is the affair of some other government to interpose itself in our problems. . . . We have some regrettable circumstances at times in our own country in which minorities are unfairly treated. We think that it is justifiable that we interfere or attempt to bring retribution to individuals or to states only because the concentration camps and the deportations were in pursuance of a common plan or enterprise of making an unjust war in which we became involved. We see no other basis on which we are justified in reaching the atrocities which were committed inside Germany, under German law, or even in violation of German law, by authorities of the German state. [7]

As a result, the anti-Jewish decrees made before the war were excluded from the case for the prosecution, even though they constituted the first stage of the Final Solution.

It is true that the United Nations General Assembly broke this artificial link between war and crimes against humanity by taking up, on its own account, the term *genocide* (coined by Raphaël Lemkin during the last months of the Nazi occupation to designate the liquidation of an ethnic group), and by adopting, on December 9, 1948, a treaty whose first article read as follows: "The contracting parties confirm that genocide, whether committed in time of peace or war, is a crime against human rights, and they pledge themselves to prevent and punish it." The problem is that in the absence of an international criminal court, the agreement foresees entrusting the state on whose territory the said genocide occurred with the task of bringing the guilty parties before their own tribunals. Which comes down to having the repression of crimes against humanity guaranteed by either the criminal (an absurd hypothesis) or the few survivors (a hypothesis that contradicts the idea of a *law* or *destiny* common to all humanity). Genocide becomes an internal affair,

55

its punishment reduced (when it takes place) to a purge, and one is thus left with the very situation that one sought to correct: the breaking up of the human race into a multitude of states.

Perhaps there is no way to remedy these gaps in international law. At least something might have happened in Lyons if they had been recognized. Instead, French justice took refuge behind the ambiguities of the judgment at Nuremberg and blurred even further the definition of crimes against humanity. Emotional thought surrendered to totalitarian thought, reintroduced under the guise of antiracism by Barbie's defenders.

We must admire the paradox: it was in reaction to Ideology that the West became so *feeling*. It is because the concern with upsetting Billancourt has lost its power of intimidation, that today we feel free enough to denounce all crimes, without drawing distinctions about their origin or finality. It is from history and its dubious sources of prestige that we have reconquered — in high combat — the gift of tears. It is the defeat of the idea of the Revolution that has enabled us to mobilize ourselves, without preliminary selection, for all the victims of inhumanity. Now, where does all this lead us, this moral liberation and this pity at last freed from restraint? To consecrate, totally unconsciously, the grand return of Ideology in the first trial to take place in France for crimes against humanity.

The problem is that, despite its vehemence and its radicalism, our critique missed the main point: Ideology is paved with good feelings. With the promise of the advent of a united and happy humanity tomorrow, relegating the diversity of opinions, interests, and conflicts born of life in society to a single Manichaean confrontation today, Ideology speaks the language of science but appeals first of all to the emotions. It flatters that part of us that cannot be resigned to the idea that plurality is the law of the earth, that part of us wishing stubbornly for a marvelously simple world where politics never strays from morality or thought from feeling, where the Other always has either the tender face of a brother or the frightening face of a killer. To be sure, excluding from the human species all those who do not belong to the family, the race, or the nation is not the same as wishing to generalize the sense of family to all humanity. But in either case — whether it is withdrawing into elementary tribalism or seeing the planet as a single and immense brotherhood — it is the law of the heart that rules, and any discord is seen as "spitting in the smiling face of brotherhood."[8]

Beyond their actual differences, either kind of totalitarian propaganda plunges us again into the idyllic and barbarous era situated by Goethe at the beginning of humanity's cultural history: everything there has "a domestic and family-oriented air about it";[9] no social relation departs from the model of intimacy; an identical, unfailing camaraderie glows on identical youthful and radiant faces.

We must, therefore, ascribe to ideology in general the definition Thomas Mann gave to National Socialism in 1940: "National Socialism means: 'I don't care about social consequences. What I want is a simple folktale.' This formulation is no doubt the mildest and the most abstract. That in reality National Socialism is also a repugnant barbarism stems from the fact that in the world of politics, fairytales turn into lies."[10]

The catastrophe of fairy tales is this: the worst kind of violence does not spring from the antagonism between men, but from the certainty of delivering them from it forever. *"Polemos,"* said Heraclitus, "is the father of all things." As Patočka powerfully demonstrates, it was to stop this reign that Ideology plunged humanity into unprecedented distress.[11] Its absolute immorality springs not from its cynicism or from its Machiavelism but from the exclusively moral nature of its categories. Its inhumane character, brought out by the prosecutor, comes from its impatient desire for fraternity. For if one admits, with Eluard, the great poet of Ideology, that "you don't need everything to make a world; you need happiness and nothing more," then is it not criminal to permit — without reacting — the militant proclaimers of unhappiness, the implacable enemies of a society that has no enemies to live and prosper?

One can conclude that humanity ceases to be humane as soon as there is no longer a place for an "enemy" in the idea it holds of itself and its destiny. Which means, *a contrario*, that *angelism is not humanism*, that discord, far from being a failure or an anachronism of society, is our most precious political good, and that the excellence of democracy, its superiority over all other forms of human coexistence, springs precisely from the fact that it institutionalized conflict by inscribing it in its guiding principles.

Now, try as we may to be henceforth — and so ardently! — democratic anti-Nazis, antitotalitarians, antifascists, antiracists and antiapartheid — we have not yet learned to be wary of the beatific smile of fraternity. In spite of Patocka, Kundera, Hannah Arendt, or Thomas Mann, the lesson of this century has not been heard: we continue to consider life in unison as the very apotheosis of being. Great legal proceedings carried out in planetary concert — this is the enchanted picture of universal sympathy that we hold up in opposition to xenophobes, to the partisans of withdrawal and the sowers of hatred. When confronted with the racist, our current object of weekly execration, we are all brothers, next-of-kin, buddies; we are all uplifted by the same feelings, our bodies move to the same rhythm of a "great Euro-world dance,"[12] our "ten billion ears"[13] are enchanted by the same harmonies, our pulses accelerate simultaneously, a like energy electrifies us, and rejecting the "old authority of verbal order"[14] in favor of a culture of sound, we sing, by the glimmer of cigarette lighters, the same hymn of hope and love across the entire face of the earth. The certainty thus spreads that if it were not for the Nazis and their epigones, all the diverse elements of humanity would melt together in an immense musical embrace.

So we cannot really blame the successive postwar generations for a general lack of memory or vigilance. Hitler, we know, but it is, alas, a kind of knowing that invests anti-Nazism with the totalitarian fantasy of transparent hearts and group happiness. To the dream of a community homogeneous in its blood and in its land, we respond by "the excessive closeness of a brotherliness that obliterate[s] all distinctions."[15] As though, in fact, nothing had happened — as though no catastrophe had cast a deathly pall over the era — the night of the idyll descends once again over humanity. Love dethrones *Polemos*, emotion invades the space of disputation and replaces the agonistic expression of opinions with the lyrical communion of persons.

Far from defending the legitimacy of *conflict* against those who seek to abolish it, we gradually lose the capacity, thus, to conceive of any other division than the exclusively moral one that separates "them" and "us" — that is, Cain and Abel. Antiracism takes the place of politics where it should only be the prerequisite for it. And it is at the moment when we congratulate ourselves on being — once and for all — rid of the blunt language of simplistic categories, that, reducing all antagonism to the cosmic and schematized combat of Light vs. Darkness, we speak that language the most ardently.

Under the guise of a great reconciliation with democratic ideals the political disappears; the moral vision of the world triumphs once again. Formerly, (that is, during the CRS-SS years), this moral vision drew its examples and slogans from the epic story of the Resistance. Today, inspired more by the martyrdom of the yellow star than by the example of the underground partisans, this vision builds on the Jewish genocide in order to impose its childishly terrible seriousness on public life as well as on culture. By virtue of Auschwitz and the call of "Never again!" (*"Plus jamais ça!"*), the value of a work now resides not in its power to reveal but in the intensity of its opposition to all discriminatory practices; not in its richness in the world but in its aptitude for purging the world of all profundity and all indeterminacy; not in its opening up to what is relative, paradoxical, ambiguous, chiaroscuro, but in the dizzying simplicity of its good sentiments. According to this point of view, from the beginning of time, poets, thinkers and writers, filmmakers, great composers and singing stars have been charged with a single and magnificent mandate: to denounce the still and forever fertile womb of racism. On television, the director of a great entertainment company confides that Baudelaire taught him tolerance. According to an anti-Heideggerian philosopher, Homer was the first to speak out against the practice of genocide. Kafka's *Metamorphosis*, we are told in countless student essays, is essentially a deeply moving parable of intolerance and exclusion, like *The Boy with Green Hair*, that very lovely film by Joseph Losey. With the best of intentions, this businessman, this philosopher, and these students rob the authors they admire (and literature in general) of everything except an edifying discourse that is pronounced, from generation to generation in ever newer guises, by some sort of perpetual Victor Hugo.

Contemporary sentiment thus makes antiracism play the same role that the Stalinist vulgate assigned to class struggle. And it is by invoking the *shoah* with indecent smugness that the aspiration to the simple folktale has today depoliticized political debate, has transformed culture into pious images, and, with no concern for the truth, has reduced the unmasterable multiplicity of mankind to an exultant face-to-face confrontation between Innocence and the Unspeakable Beast.

CHAPTER NINE

THE CORRUPTION
OF THE EVENT

Taking refuge behind the façade of the folktale, Ideology thus resurfaced in the very place where it should have been called to account. This is the paradox that stupefied Mr. Zaoui, and that he wished to point out, in a gesture that was itself provocative and exceptional. A waste of time! Multiple handicaps prevented him from being heard: Jewish, he was a priori suspected of pleading for his own constituency; relatively unknown, he indulged in the rare, unheard-of scandal of not allying himself with the celebrities at the bar; finally — the ultimate stroke against him — he was one of the thirty-nine lawyers whose thirty-nine closing speeches talked the audience into a stupor without interruption from the 17th to the 26th of June. The irritation building up against the plaintiffs in the course of the hearing was unleashed on Mr. Zaoui when he tried to interrupt his Algerian colleague: "Enough, you windbags! Shut up! We have already heard more than enough from you! You have expounded shamelessly for eight days; you are not going to add to this by drowning out the voice of your opponents!" Such was the spontaneous cry that greeted and ended, without further ado, his protest. The allegations of Mr. Bouaïta had no importance in this context. Perhaps he was *excessive,* but the opposing counsel came from the *boring* camp, and this unforgivable membership was enough to disqualify his behavior.

We have come a long way since the era when Péguy the journalist could still propose to "tell the truth, the whole truth, nothing but the truth, stupidly the stupid truth, boringly the boring truth, sadly the sad truth."[1] In the meantime, the event has passed from the domain of *history* into the sphere of *entertainment:* what constitutes an event is not its terms of action or of circumstance but its presentation; it's not the thing that happens, it's the clever headline that can be made from it, or the "scoop," that puts it in the limelight.

Whether it amuses or moves us, the event henceforth has as its primary mission to entertain, not to concern: "Starring this Summer — Peace" ran the headline in a large Parisian paper, to appropriately mark the concurrent retreat of Soviet troops from Afghanistan and the cease-fire between Iraq and Iran. Farewell, Péguy; except for a few little pockets of resistance, themselves more and more under attack, the austere concern for the truth has progressively given way to the need to make "coups" and to keep the public in a state of breathlessness. The principle of objectivity, which had succeeded in resisting pressure from state policy and from the sophistry of partisan logic, has unconditionally abdicated before the unbridled will to "spice up" information (as one does a recipe) in order to beat out the competition and attract customers. And, with politics giving way entirely to game-playing, there is no such thing anymore as a "boring" event. It would be a contradiction in terms. As though the event were still a category of the world, whereas it is heading inexorably toward becoming a diversion with set hours — like a category of life.

For several wrong reasons — including inexperience, the

need to be visible, and personal rivalries, but also because an unpaid debt to the dead bound them to the truth — the lawyers for the one hundred and forty-six plaintiffs (associations and individual victims) were not able to adapt themselves to this great ontological mutation of the event. Duty-bound by the past, weighted down by "that which, at one time, was,"[2] they could resort to the easy tricks of eloquence (and some of them, alas, did not hesitate to do so), but not to sensationalism. Instead of moving quickly, they were interminable. Instead of making an impression, they made people yawn. Rather than satisfying the appetite for the new, they rehashed, ad nauseam, the same tired formulas. Mr. Zaoui paid the price of condemnation without appeal for this serious breach of the media's laws of the event.

Mr. Vergès, on the other hand, was free. No debt tied him to the past; he was in a position to plant suspense in the very heart of the ceremony of remembering and to substitute the delicious thrill of the event for the meticulous reassessment of the facts. With him, everything became possible: even that the past could cease to be unalterable — that is, bothersome — even the retrospective *coup de théâtre*, even the emergence of a heart-stirring truth beneath the monotony of official truth. Hence the constant flattering attention paid to him, which contrasted with the excessive scorn shown to "the swarming, disorganized mob"[3] of his adversaries.

It is true that this ascendancy did not imply any adherence to him. Mr. Vergès attracted attention; he did not exercise influence. Rejected as a fanatic, he was only sought out as a kind of condiment. It was not the doctrinarian in him that captivated attention, it was the showman who entertained the public. He was not the activist who scored points but the devil who made the show more lively. It was not the radical nature of his cause

65

that aroused enthusiasm, it was his promise of scandal, his steamy reputation, and his consummate art of mystery that inspired envy: "In war as in justice, the trump card lies in believing in nothing, in calculating from a distance a cold strategy, at a bird's-eye view, in being emblazoned with the infamy that this apparent inhumanity arouses."[4] Morally detested for the substance of his claims, the lawyer of "Don Klaus"[5] was adulated in the media for the same imperious and superficial reasons that had earlier prompted the German magazine *Stern* to publish the alleged "secret notebooks" of Hitler. Vergès incarnated a hope that was no more militant than the plea addressed by a journalist to Barbie as the latter left his box to absent himself from the trial — that he give him (as an exclusive) the name of the traitor who had betrayed Jean Moulin to the German police. Such a success could not fail to result in a stay of proceedings for his beneficiary. If Vergès didn't keep his promises, he would be thrown to the lions; even if he kept them, life was too insatiable to be grateful to him for it. For as soon as an event has slaked our thirst for surprise, life turns away and looks elsewhere for new novelties, for other events of the century. The information is there, as are all the cultural industries, to provide us with endless different subjects. "Don't bore the folks; quick, something else."[6] In the age of entertainment, "news" has usurped the place of historicity; moments no longer follow one another according to a reasoned and recountable order; they succeed one another like meals in an unending cycle. With the world transformed into a multiform and permanent object of consumption, its destiny is to be continually gobbled up by its consumers.

Today a lot of people see in this divorce between audience and influence our best guarantee against the murderous tendencies of Ideology. Ideology, they say, can go ahead and return to Lyons, but it is undercut by the very interest it arouses. Since the age of entertainment is that of short-lived excitements, since, as Régis Debray writes, "Now, everything is now,"[7] everything is instant, everything comes into view only to disappear, there is then nothing to worry about: democracy has finally become insubvertible, no lasting military call-to-arms can hold out against the feverish round of news flashes, of catastrophes, of great moments. To the great detriment of recruiting officers on all sides, the spirit of "system" has no hold on the man filled with disparate bits of information. Sentimentality itself has been transformed into brief infatuations that are too unsustained to provoke any fear of sentimental excess. And since the purpose of the event is no longer to be *memorable* but to be *disposable* — so that as soon as it has appeared and been consumed it gives way, with no fuss and no history, to the next one — those who *make* the event (Vergès included) die with the event they create.

It remains to be seen if we can really count only on the whims of the news media to exorcise the ravages of the heart, and if the only way history can avoid being shackled by a "scientific" law is for humanity to have no more history — only an eternal present of current events. Civilization established the Nuremberg Trials in order to *bring the law to justice* by denouncing its fraudulent ideological and disciplinary imitations. We abandon this ambition if we allow entertainment to release humanity from continuity, from coherence, and from all forms of the law.

CHAPTER TEN

WHEN THE WORLD
ENTERS THE HOME

At the end of this trial that was unanimously hailed as exemplary, certain religious and moral leaders expressed a single (small) regret — that the debates had not been televised. In fact, as we know, after a long and tumultuous debate, it was decided to film the proceedings, with the proviso that this archival footage be shown only after thirty years. Those who did not support the compromise solution handed down by Robert Badinter defended their impatience by invoking the extraordinary nature of the trial. An exception should be made, they maintained, for this out-of-the-ordinary event. Since, for the first time in France, a man was being judged for crimes against humanity, there was no valid reason, in an age when technology had broken down all physical barriers, to leave humanity outside of the closed quarters where the judicial action — taken in its name — was going on. The great anti-Nazi lesson meted out in Lyons could thereby benefit everyone. Instead of being limited to a chosen minority or filtered through the subjectivity of journalists, the appalling testimonies of Lise Lesèvre, Simone Lagrange, and the two mothers of Izieu, Mesdames Halaunbrenner and Benguigui would enter directly, immediately, into

all homes, without losing their emotional impact en route. And
that would perhaps have prevented the scene, one year later, of
four million French voters giving their voices to a man who
openly declares that the responsibilities for World War II are
divided and that the existence of the gas chambers should not
be considered "revealed truth" since "historians debate these
questions."[1] Could one, in fact, imagine a more effective anti-
dote than the trial of a former chief of the Gestapo for discredit-
ing the aggressively "revisionist" arguments of the new extreme
Right?

This confidence in the pedagogical and therapeutic virtues of
the television screen is based on a postulate: that television is a
neutral instrument, a simple means of communication that has
no effect on the subject matter it transmits. However, following
a trial in the courtroom is not the same thing as watching it at
home in your armchair. In the courtroom, you can't telephone
or do busy work or flop down or help your children with their
homework — or even munch an apple. "Court is in session!":
bodily functions have to be brought under control, the drone of
daily life has to be suspended so that the judicial ceremony can
unfold. The same principle holds true, in fact, for justice as for
religion, for theater or for the act of teaching — it can be done
anywhere (a table suffices), but only by isolating the time and
the space of these interactions from their secular settings.
Therefore it is doubly absurd to want to televise judicial proceedings in order to educate people. For far from reproducing
this fundamental *separation*, television presents the sacred as
food for the secular, and puts the outside world at the mercy of
the private world. Under the guise of having the world enter the
home, television allows the home to impose itself on the world.
No work is admirable enough, no catastrophe terrible enough,
no word edifying enough to make us stop eating our apple or

talking back to the screen. With television, the drone of life triumphs over every interruption — *life is never silent.* It is no longer man who must step outside the eternal round of needs and satisfactions and tear himself from his life (biological, private, day-to-day) in order to make himself available to the world's humanity; the human world is delivered to his home, and is put at the disposal of life, just like the apple. It is no longer the Don Quixote in us who must silence Sancho Panza, it is Sancho Panza who alone occupies the whole terrain, and who enjoys his omnipotence.[2]

Carried to its conclusion, such a reversal implies the disappearance of justice, of schools, of theater:

> The very atmosphere of drama is *silence.* The more powerful this silence, the more rebellious, the more intense the dramatic effect that attacks and destroys it. Drama begins with silence, just as it ends with it. It steps out from it in order to return to it. It is like a rupture, a brief awakening, like a discordant exclamation between two borders of silence.[3]

Such a reversal implies, more generally, the disappearance of everything that transcends the maintenance or the reproduction of daily life. This is why there are things that are not yet televisable, like the trial at Lyons — despite the pressure from people of great conscience.

It is true that these people are right about one thing: forty-five years after the Liberation, France cannot allow a demagogue's promoting the denial of the gas chambers to the status of a separate school of historical thought to go unchallenged, and his combating (with a virulence untouched by the experience of this century) the idea that our neighbor is not limited to those close to us but includes all the inhabitants of the earth. For the rest, by encouraging the media to violate the last sanctuaries still protected from its rule, in order to triumph over exclusion, our humanists are not serving the cause of humanity. They are merely adding the soul of antiracism to rampant mediazation. They see their close adhesion to an irresistible movement as an act of resistance, and under the pretext of ending barbarism, they hasten our entry into an era where nothing that men have gained through hard work will escape the fate of the apple — that is, consumption.

And even if they failed in this particular case, given the definition of the event that prevailed throughout the proceedings and the way in which boredom was penalized, it can be said that the eye of the television audience preceded the cameras; for *reality* now tends to be lived as *a possibility* passing improperly for a single program, like a stupidly necessary image, like a big, interminable, and bland apple that we — frustrated channel switchers — tolerate less and less for not being able to exchange, during the show, for some more heady pleasure.

CHAPTER ELEVEN

THE REMOVAL OF SCRUPLES; OR, THE OTHER STROKE OF MIDNIGHT

"For every man and every event," said Péguy, as we recall, "there comes a moment, an hour; an hour strikes when they become historic; a certain stroke of midnight sounds on a certain village clock tower when the real event passes over into history."

The Barbie trial did in fact delay the moment, "the stroke of midnight," when the victims of Nazism would pass over from the real into the historic. But that stroke — cruel irony — lent a kind of aura or prescribed urgency to the already quasi-total takeover of human life by consumption and sentimentality. As though the century's memory commanded us to forget its lessons. As though Auschwitz, no less, obliged us to translate everything through the media, without discretion or scruple. As though, in a word, the very voice of the dead begged us to put the world to our uses instead of opening ourselves up to it, and told us to transform history, in its entirety, into a children's story.

73

Notes

1. History's Last Summons

1. Charles Péguy, "A nos amis, à nos abonnés," in *Oeuvres en prose, 1909–1914* (Paris: Gallimard, 1957), pp. 45 and 48.

2. Ibid., p. 48.

2. The Legality of Evil

1. Max Picard, *L'homme du néant* [*Hitler in uns selbst*], tr. Jean Rousset (Paris: La Balconnière, 1947), p. 49.

2. Edgar Faure, Introduction to *La Persécution des Juifs en France et dans les autres pays de l'Ouest* (Paris: Center of Contemporary Jewish Documentation, 1947), pp. 22 and 21.

3. Ibid., p. 29.

4. Ibid., p. 31.

5. Eugène Aroneanu, *Le crime contre l'humanité* (Paris: Dalloz, 1961).

6. Montesquieu, *De l'esprit des lois*, 2 vols. (Paris: Garnier Flammarion, 1979), book 26, 2:177.

7. D'Holbach, quoted in Reiner Koselleck, *La règne de la critique* (Paris: Editions de Minuit, 1975), p. 35.

8. Quoted in Henri Meyrowitz, *La répression par les tribunaux allemands des crimes contre l'humanité et de l'appartenance à une organisation criminelle* (Paris: LGDJ, 1960), p. 180.

9. Faure, Introduction, p. 32.

10. Jacques Vergès, *Je défends Barbie* (Paris: Jean Piccolec, 1988), p. 22.

3. The Quid pro Quo

1. Hannah Arendt, *Eichmann in Jerusalem* (New York: Viking, 1963), p. 270.

2. The Moscow Declaration, quoted in Jacques-Bernard Herzog, *Nuremberg: un echec fructueux?* (Paris: Librairie générale de droit et de jurisprudence, 1975), p. 50.

3. Edgar Faure, Introduction to *La Persécution des Juifs en France et dans les autres pays de l'Ouest* (Paris: Center of Contemporary Jewish Documentation, 1947), p. 32

4. Eberhard Jackel, *Devant L'histoire, Les documents de la controverse sur la singularité de l'extermination des Juifs par le régime nazi* (Paris: Cerf, 1988), pp. 97–98.

5. Saul Friedlander, "Reflexions sur l'historisation du national-socialisme" in *Vingtième siecle* (Presses de la fondation nationale des sciences politiques), October-December 16, 1987, p. 54.

6. Hannah Arendt, *Eichmann in Jerusalem*, p. 279.

4. Hero and Victim

1. Primo Levi, *The Truce*, tr. Stuart Woolf, in *If This is a Man* and *The Truce* (London: Penguin, 1979), p. 226.

2. Henry Rousso, *Le syndrome de Vichy* (Paris: Seuil, 1987), p. 35.

3. Ibid., p. 179.

4. These words were spoken during a seminar on "The Nazi Politics of Extermination," held at the Sorbonne, December 11–13, 1987.

5. Jean-Marc Théolleyre, "Crimes de guerre et crimes contre l'humanité," in *Le Procès de Klaus Barbie, Le Monde* (special edition), July 1987, p. 6.

6. Article 6b of the Statute of the International Military Tribunal describes the following as being acts of war: "the killing, ill-treatment, or deportation, for forced labor or for other ends, of civilian populations in occupied territories, the killing or ill-treatment of prisoners of war or of people at sea, the execution of hostages, the looting of public or private property, the unprovoked destruction of towns and villages, or any destruction that cannot be attributed to military necessity."
Article 6c puts the following in the category of crimes against humanity: "the killing, extermination, enslavement, deportation, and all inhuman acts committed against any civil populations, before or dur-

ing the war, or else persecutions for political, racial, or religious motives when these acts or persecutions — whether or not they may have
constituted a violation of the domestic law of the country where they
were perpetrated — were committed following any crime under the jurisdiction of the tribunal or in connection with that crime." Henri
Meyrowitz, *La répression par les tribunaux allemands*, pp. 480–481.

7.   Edgar Faure, Introduction, p. 28.

8.   André Frossard, *Le crime contre l'humanité* (Paris: Laffont, 1987).

9.   Hearing of May 25, 1987, quoted by Jean-Marie Théolleyre,
"Crimes de guerre," p. 10.

10.   Hearing of June 3, 1987, Ibid., p. 22.

11.   René Char, *Fureur et mystère* (Paris: Gallimard, 1967), pp. 137–
138.

12.   Hearing of June 3, 1987, quoted in *Procès Barbie, l'Agence France
Presse raconte* (Paris: Agence France Press), p. 142.

13.   Hearing of July 3, 1987, quoted in Théolleyre, "Crimes de
guerre," p. 40.

5. White Inmates, White Executioners

1.   Arthur Schopenhauer. *Le monde comme volonté et comme repré-
sentation* (Paris: Presses Universitaires de France, 1966), p. 1222;
E. F. J. Payne, tr., *The World as Will and Representation* (Falcon's Wing,
1958).

2.   Pascal, "Préface au Traité du vide," in *De l'esprit géométrique, Ecrits
sur la Grâce et autres textes* (Paris: GF-Flammarion, 1985), p. 62.

3.   Pascal, *Pensées*, no. 210, ed. Brunschvicg (Paris: Garnier, 1964),
p. 131.

4.   Pascal, "Préface au Traité du vide," p. 62.

5.   I borrow this expression from Walter Benjamin's *Thèses sur la phi-
losophie de l'histoire*.

6.   Theodor Adorno, *Minima Moralia* (Paris: Payot, 1980), p. 218;
E.F.N. Jephcott, tr., *Minima Moralia* (London: NLB, 1974).

7.   Edgar Faure, Introduction to *La Persécution des Juifs en France et*

∂anƆ leɔ autreɔ payɔ ∂e l'OueƆt (Paris: Center of Contemporary Jewish Documentation, 1947), p. 24.

8. Paul Valéry. "La crise de l'esprit," in Variété I (Paris: Gallimard, 1978), p. 15.

9. "Reason can't linger over the wounds inflicted on individuals, for individual destinies are swallowed up in the universal destiny." Hegel, La raiɔon ∂anƆ l'Hiɔtoire (Paris: Union Generale D'Editions, 1965), p. 68; Robert S. Hartman, tr., ReaƆon in Hiɔtory (Indianapolis: Bobbs-Merrill, 1953).

10. V. Jankélévitch, L'ImpréɔcriptibƖe (Paris: Seuil, 1986), p. 43.

11. Quoted by Shulamit Volkov, in L'Allemagne nazie et le génocide juif, Colloquium at the Ecole des Hautes Etudes en Sciences Sociales (Paris: Gallimard-Seuil, 1985), p. 83.

12. Primo Levi, Survival in AuƆchwitz, tr. Stuart Woolf (New York: Collier-MacMillan, 1961), p. 96. First published as If Thiɔ iɔ a Man (New York: Orion, 1959).

13. Levi, Survival in AuƆchwitz, p. 96.

14. Ilya Ehrenbourg, La RuƆɔie en guerre (Paris: Gallimard, 1968), pp. 45–46; Gerard Shelley, tr., RuƆɔia at War (London: H. Hamilton, 1943).

15. Hearing of July 1, 1987.

16. I borrow this expression from Hannah Arendt, who uses it in several of her works, notably in Men in Dark TimeƆ (New York: Harcourt, Brace, World, 1968).

17. Marcel Merle, Le ProcèƆ ∂e Nuremberg et le châtiment ∂eƆ criminelƆ ∂e guerre (Paris: Pedonc, 1949), p. 158.

18. Of course we had to wait until the sixties to see this struggle culminate and result in equal rights. But it was in November 1945 — that is, scarcely six months after the unconditional surrender of the German army — that the American Jewish Congress created a Commission on Law and Social Action with a view toward helping all those who suffered from discrimination. Thus, President Truman rightly noted in his MemoirƆ: "Hitler's persecution of the Jews did much to awaken Americans to the dangerous extremes to which prejudice can

be carried if allowed to control government actions." Quoted in Raul Hilberg, *The Destruction of the European Jews* (Chicago: Quadrangle Books, 1961), p. 761.

19. Paul Ricoeur, *Le Temps raconté, Temps et Récit III* (Paris: Seuil, 1985), p. 273.

20. "If we Algerians are to have any place whatsoever in this trial, it is not as witnesses for the defense, on behalf of Barbie, but as witnesses for the prosecution, in the name of the rights of Man that legitimize our own struggle." Hocine Ait Ahmed and Mohammed Harbi, in *Le Nouvel Observateur*, no. 1183, July 10, 1987.

21. Jacques Vergès, *Je défends Barbie* (Paris: Jean Piccolec, 1988), p. 13.

22. For example, here is what one could read in the section devoted to the Barbie trial in the weekly newspaper *Algérie-Actualité* (no. 1127, week of May 21–27, 1987) entitled, bluntly, "What do Jews Want?"

More than forty years later, the Holocaust is causing a furor. As soon as a Jew starts to cry somewhere in this vast world, humanity is accused of being basically anti-Semitic, and, one after the other, History and the men who made it are dragged in.

The Holocaust is the Jewish flame of Olympus, maintained by a world-wide financial power, with the aid of the media.

How can you tell Palestinians to commit to memory the dramas of the past, when they are living through far more unbearable ones? What difference is there between a gas chamber and a cluster bomb that falls on an Arab house on a night of Ramadan?

What can you say to Palestinian children about the common foundations of humanity if one day the men who deprived them of memories don't suffer the infamy of being in the dock of the accused? While awaiting brotherly love, which has been sublimated like death, there exists this truth. The truth of Mr. Jacques Vergès, "anti-Semite" in spite of himself, surrounded by the insulting slogans of these fanatics of persecution: "The Zionists go so far back in time that they assume the aspect of Teutonic knights."

6. The Incident

1. Jacques Vergès, *Pour en finir avec Ponce-Pilate* (Paris: Pré-aux-Clercs, 1983), p. 23.

2. Ibid., p. 24.

3. Quoted by Henri Noguères, in *La vérité aura le dernier mot* (Paris: Seuil, 1985), p. 233.

4. Jacques Vergès, in Jacques Vergès and Etienne Bloch, *La face cachée du procès Barbie* (Paris: Samuel Tastet, 1983), pp. 66 and 17.

5. Hearing of June 23, 1987.

6. Bernard-Henri Lévy, *Archives d'un procès Klaus Barbie* (Paris: Le Livre de Poche, 1987), p. 9.

7. Hearing of July 1, 1987.

8. *Libération,* July 6, 1987.

9. A few months later, a journalist from *Libération* saw "a certain justification in the questions asked by Jacques Vergès" in the way in which France accommodated itself to the assault on the cave at Ouvéa. Nineteen New Caledonian independence militants were killed by French soldiers charged with liberating the hostages these men had taken after an attack on a police barracks that had left four dead; it did not appear that this carnage would be the subject of legal action. What could this journalist conclude, democratically committed as he was to equality in life as well as in death, if not that twenty Canaques killed in a military operation constituted an "unfortunate mistake" because they were black, whereas six million Jews murdered by the Nazis, without any military or strategic motive, are victims of a crime against *humanity* because they are European. In other words, Vergès was right; his closing speech was premonitory, and "one could easily imagine the rejoicing of Barbie's lawyer if a trial of the soldiers accused of setting a 'death mission' in motion opened tomorrow, and if, as the plaintiff, he represented the families of the victims. Suddenly his claims about 'the pot calling the kettle black' and his refusal to admit the right of the French justice system to judge Barbie before cleaning up the mess of its own colonial past, would be legitimized in the public's eyes." Francis Zamponi, "Vergès vu d'Ouvéa," *Libération,* May 16, 1988.

7. Emotional Confusion

1. Hearing of June 29, 1987.

2. Hearing of June 29, 1987, quoted by Jean-Marie Théolleyre, "Crimes de guerre et crimes contre l'humanité," in *Le Procès de Klaus Barbie, Le Monde* (special edition), July 1987, p. 37.

3. Hearing of June 26, 1987, ibid., p. 35.

4. Jacques Vergès, *Je défends Barbie* (Paris: Jean Piccolec, 1988).

8. The Night of the Idyll

1. Hannah Arendt, *The Origins of Totalitarianism*, 2d ed. (Cleveland: World Publishing, 1958), p. 469.

2. Ibid., p. 464.

3. Ibid., p. 465.

4. Max Picard, *L'homme du néant [Hitler in uns selbst]*, tr. Jean Rousset (Paris: La Balconnière, 1947), p. 191.

5. *Le procès de Nuremberg, Le verdict* (Paris: Office français d'édition, 1947).

6. Quoted and discussed in Henri Meyrowitz, *La répression par les tribunaux allemands des crimes contre l'humanité et de l'appartenance à une organisation criminelle* (Paris: LGDJ, 1960), p. 18.

7. Quoted in Raul Hilberg, *The Destruction of the European Jews* (Chicago: Quadrangle Books, 1961), pp. 686–687.

8. Milan Kundera, *L'insoutenable légèreté de l'être* (Paris: Gallimard, 1983), p. 316; Michael Henry Heim, tr., *The Unbearable Lightness of Being* (New York: Harper and Row), 1984.

9. Goethe, "Les époques de la culture sociale" [1832], in *Ecrits sur l'Art*, tr. and ed. by Jean-Marie Schaeffer (Klincksieck, 1983); Ellen von Nordroff and Ernest H. von Nordroff, tr., John Gearey, ed., *Essays on Art and Literature* (New York: Suhrkamp Publishers, 1986).

10. Thomas Mann, "Défense de Wagner," in *Wagner et notre temps* (Paris: Pluriel, 1978), p. 178.

11. Jan Patočka, *Essais hérétiques* (Paris: Verdier, 1981).

12. Jean-François Bizot, *Libération*, June 18–19, 1989 (speaking

about the triple concert Paris–New York–Dakar organized by SOS Racism to mark the anniversary of June 18, 1988).

13. I borrow this expression from the advertising campaign of Megastore, the large record store opened by Virgin Records in October 1988 on the Champs-Elysées in Paris.

14. George Steiner, *In Bluebeard's Castle: Some Notes Toward the Redefinition of Culture* (New Haven: Yale University Press, 1971), p. 118.

15. Hannah Arendt, *Men in Dark Times* (New York: Harcourt, Brace, World, 1968), p. 30.

9. The Corruption of the Event

1. Charles Péguy, "Lettre du Provincial," *Oeuvres en prose complètes,* ed. Robert Burac, 2 vols. (Paris: Gallimard, 1987), 1:291–292.

2. Paul Ricoeur, *Le Temps raconté, Temps et Récit III* (Paris: Seuil, 1985), p. 204.

3. With the precision of a novelistic imagination, Bertrand Poirot-Delpech attributes this expression to Barbie, in *Monsieur Barbie n'a rien à dire* (Paris: Gallimard, 1987), p. 31. But during interruptions in the hearings, journalists expressed their exasperation in similar language. The Nazi loathing of vermin and the channel-switching "zapper"'s distaste for repetition were thus — fleetingly — conjoined.

4. Betrand Poirot-Delpech, *Monsieur Barbie,* p. 35.

5. This is, in fact, the title (conveying a deferential sympathy) that Mr. Vergès uses hereafter for his most famous client, *Beauté du crime* (Paris: Plon, 1988), *passim.*

6. Gilles Lipovetsky, *L'empire de l'éphémère* (Paris: Gallimard, 1987), p. 251.

7. Régis Debray, *Le pouvoir intellectuel en France* (Paris: Gallimard, 1986, p. 128).

10. When the World Enters the Home

1. Jean-Marie Le Pen, "Grand Jury RTL," *Le Monde,* Sept. 13, 1987. Let it be said in passing that this implicit acknowledgment of Faurisson reveals clearly that by presenting the gas chambers as "a

minor detail in the history of World War II," Jean-Marie Le Pen cast suspicion on the very reality of the genocide, and showed no sign of what he later protested with all the vehemence of a just man — his compassion for all the victims, whatever their nationality or the weapons and means used to destroy them. By concentrating their indignation on the single word "detail," the news commentators unconsciously facilitated the defense and reestablishment of the man they thought they finally had a grip on.

2.   By broadcasting *Shoah* late in the evening — that is, at an hour when daily activity has wound down, television's channel 1 unwittingly outsmarted this fatal secularization. The motives of the programmers were purely commercial (to avoid taking risks during prime time), but their cynicism protected Lanzmann's film from our everyday environment and domestic activities — instead of letting it be drowned out by them — as is the usual case with television.

3.   Jacques Copeau, *Registres I, Appels* (Paris: Gallimard, 1974), p. 162.

Glossary

Birth and death dates are provided where possible.

Ait Ahmed, Hocine (b. 1926). Kabyl leader of the exterior delegation of the FLN (Algerian National Liberation Front) imprisoned by the French from 1956 to 1962. Elected to first Algerian assembly, but entered into conflict with Ben Bella (president of the Algerian Republic from 1963–1965), and created an opposition party, Le Front des Forces Socialistes. Arrested in 1964; escaped from Algeria in 1966; lives in exile in Europe. He and Mohammed Harbi, another former FLN leader, spoke against Vergès.

Arendt, Hannah (1906–1975). German-born Jew who fled Nazi Germany in 1933. Political refugee in the U.S. from 1940 until her death. Philosopher and political theorist best known for *The Origins of Totalitarianism* (1951) and *Eichmann in Jerusalem* (1963).

Auschwitz. Largest concentration and extermination camp in the Nazi territories; located at Auschwitz, Poland, in the Upper Silesian industrial region. Prisoners used as forced labor and gassed. Between one million and one and a half million people died there.

Badinter, Robert (b. 1928). Minister of justice under François Mitterand (1981–1986); arranged for Barbie's extradition. His father, Simon Badinter, arrested in a raid by Barbie on the

Jewish welfare office [UGIF] in February 1943, perished at Auschwitz.

Bal, Claude. French filmmaker charged with defaming the French Resistance in *Que la vérité est amère* (The bitter truth), a documentary about René Hardy, the man accused of having betrayed Jean Moulin to the Nazis.

Billancourt. Reference to Boulogne-Billancourt, industrial neighborhood in the southwest of Paris, synonymous with the communist trade union CGT (Conféderation Générale du Travail).

Birkenau. Part of Auschwitz extermination camp, also known as Auschwitz II. Housed 150,000 prisoners.

Bormann, Martin (1900–1945). Staff leader of the Nationalsozialistiszhe Deutsche Arbeiterpartei (National Socialist German Worker's Party), head of the party bureau. Executor of National Socialist racial programs. As of 1943 official "secretary to the Fuhrer" and Hitler's closest confidant. Sentenced to death in absentia at Nuremberg; committed suicide by cyanide in 1945.

Bouaïta, Nabil. Algerian attorney, member of the Klaus Barbie defense team.

Caluire. Suburb of Lyons (once a Roman village) where Jean Moulin was arrested in a clandestine meeting with other Resistance leaders on June 21, 1943.

Char, René (1907–1988). French poet, participated as chief of a Resistance *maquis* (armed, clandestine resistance groups organizing from French hills and mountains) during the Occupation.

86

CRS-SS years. Reference to the 1960s. CRS (Compagnie Républicaine de Sécurité) are the French security police who controlled public demonstrations during the 1960s. The chant, "CRS-SS," compared them with Hitler's SS.

Debray, Regis (b. 1941). Took part in guerrilla war in Latin America alongside Che Guevara; arrested in Bolivia and sentenced to thirty years detention; liberated in December 1970. Adviser to Mitterand since 1981; participated, with Serge Klarsfeld, in an attempt to extradite Barbie in 1972–73. Author of *Le pouvoir intellectual en France* (1986).

Deir Yassin. Palestinian village, attacked by a contingent from the Revisionist Zionist Irgun and Stern Gang groups on April 9, 1948, before the founding declaration of the State of Israel. Three hundred people died in the attack, which was officially denounced by Ben-Gurion and the Israeli leadership.

Dontenwille, Henri. Deputy director of Public Prosecution, involved in decision to expand the French definition of "crimes against humanity" to include political prosecution and thus to try Klaus Barbie for his actions against the Resistance.

Dreyfus, Alfred (1859–1935). French Jewish army officer framed for treason, condemned, and then cleared in a series of trials that inflamed anti-Semitic nationalism and polarized French public opinion.

Durkheim, Emile (1858–1917). French sociologist and philosopher; one of the founders and leading figures in modern sociology.

Eichmann, Adolf (1906–1962). Central figure in deportation of over three million Jews to death camps; SS officer; head of the Jewish Evacuation Department of the Gestapo. Escaped American captivity in 1946; fled with church assistance to Argentina. Tried and sentenced by Israelis; executed on May 31, 1962.

Ehrenbourg, Ilya (1891–1967). Soviet Jew, author, journalist; worked in Western Europe during the thirties and World War II as a correspondent for Soviet newspapers.

Faure, Edgar (b. 1908). French political figure; appointed by De Gaulle in 1945 as assistant delegate to the French jurists participating in the War Crimes Trials.

Frank, Hans (1900–1946). Leading jurist of the Nazi party. As Governor-General of Poland during World War II, led the extermination of Poles and Polish Jews; executed as a war criminal at Nuremberg in 1946.

Friedlander, Saul (b. 1932). Czech Jew, author of *When Memory Comes* (Farrar, Straus, 1979), a memoir about coming of age in France at the end of the Holocaust and his later life in Jerusalem.

Fritsch, Theodor (1852–1933). German author of *The Anti-Semite's Catechism* (1910), first published in Germany in 1887 under the pseudonym Thomas Frey.

Frossard, André (b. 1915). French journalist known for religious writings; a member of the French Academy since 1987. Opposed the inclusion of crimes against the Resistance in the French definition of crimes against humanity.

Gide, André (1869–1951). French novelist, critic, essayist, dramatist; awarded Nobel Prize in 1947. His *Travels in the Congo* (1927) is an exposé of colonial policies in Africa.

Goering, Hermann (1893–1946). Reichstag president in 1932; head of the Gestapo and Luftwaffe; title was Reichemarschall. Morphine addict. Sentenced to death at Nuremberg; committed suicide.

Grossman, Vassili (1905–1964). Russian Jewish engineer, journalist, author; reporter for the Soviet Defense Ministry's newspaper during World War II. His *Life and Fate* (translated into English in 1986) draws upon his wartime experience. The Communist Party's Central Committee confiscated all but one copy of the book, which survived on microfilm. Grossmann was spared deportation or execution by Stalin's death in 1953.

Himmler, Heinrich (1900–1945). SS leader and head of the Nazi state security apparatus. Organizer of mass murder. Committed suicide during an attempt to escape through British lines.

Hugo, Victor (1802–1885). French novelist, poet, playwright at the forefront of the Romantic movement. Elected to the French academy in 1841; forced into exile in 1851 for actively opposing Louis Napoleon.

International Convention on Laws and War Customs, The Hague. On September 7, 1907, it ruled that world powers must give advance declaration of war.

Izieu. Farm town near Lyons; location of children's home that harbored Jewish children who were deported by Klaus Barbie in 1944, never to return.

Jackson, Robert H. (1892–1954). Appointed by Truman in 1945 to represent the United States in negotiations for war crime trials; later named chief counsel for the United States at the trials.

Jankélévitch, Vladimir (1903–1985). French philosopher, educator, author, and music critic; an important figure in French existentialism.

Jaspers, Karl (1883–1969). An important and influential German-born existentialist philosopher.

89

Kaltenbrunner, Ernst (1903–1946). Head of Austrian SS after 1935. Director of Reich Security Main Office and chief of security police and SD as of 1943 (superior of Eichmann); prime mover of the Final Solution in last two years of the war. Executed by hanging.

Khmer Rouge. Left-wing Cambodian insurgent group whose 1974–75 offensive resulted in the creation of Democratic Kampuchea, with Pol Pot as the head of government. The regime entered into a two-year armed conflict with Vietnam. The Khmer Rouge attempted to impose rural communism by violent and repressive means; urban populations were forced into exile, educated and middle classes systematically exterminated along with all other perceived enemies of the regime; economic life destroyed. By 1979, two million had died as a result of Khmer Rouge policy in what has become known as an *autogenocide*. Vietnam invaded in 1979; Pol Pot was overthrown by the Front Uni de Salut National du Kampuchéa (F.U.N.S.K.).

Klarsfeld, Beate (b. 1939) and Serge (b. 1935). International investigators who have identified former Nazi war criminals and worked to bring them to justice. Played a role in the location and extradition of Klaus Barbie. Serge Klarsfeld appeared at the Barbie trial as an attorney for a *partie civile*.

Kundera, Milan (b. 1929). Czech writer and critic of totalitarianism whose plays were banned and whose books were removed from libraries in his own country. Author of *The Book of Laughter and Forgetting* (1979) and *The Unbearable Lightness of Being*. Naturalized French citizen since 1981.

Lanzmann, Claude (b. 1925). Journalist and filmmaker. Member of the postwar existentialist culture with Sartre and Beauvoir (wrote for *Les Temps modernes*). In 1985, produced and directed *Shoah*, a nine and a half hour documentary film about the Holocaust.

Lemkin, Raphaël. Polish-born lecturer on international law at Yale and "father" of the antigenocide pact. Coined the term *genocide,* which could refer to acts of wartime and peacetime; asked the League of Nations to outlaw genocide in 1933. His definition was adopted by UN General Assembly in 1948 and is known as the Lemkin Resolution.

Le Pen, Jean-Marie (b. 1928). Leader of the right-wing nationalist party in France, le Front National. In the first round of the 1988 French presidential elections he won 14.44 percent of the vote. President of the National Front since 1972; elected to the European parliament in 1984, represented the Front national de Paris as a deputy in the French parliament from 1986–88. In a September 1987 interview, Le Pen referred to the gas chambers of the Nazi death camps as a "detail" in the history of World War II and voiced doubts about the number of Jews exterminated by the Nazis.

Lesèvre, Lise (b. 1905). Member of French Resistance; arrested with her husband and son, who did not survive. Tortured by Klaus Barbie in thirteen separate interrogations. Author of *Face à Barbie: Souvenirs-cauchemars de Montluc à Ravensbruck* (Paris: Nouvelles Editions du Pavillon, 1987), recounting her experience.

Lessing, Gotthold Ephraïm (1729–1781). German writer, moralist, and dramatist; author of *L'Education du genre humain* (1780).

Levi, Primo (1919–1987). Italian chemist, survivor of Auschwitz-Birkenau; author of memoirs. Committed suicide in April 1987.

Lévy, Bernard-Henri (b. 1948). French intellectual of the group known as the "new philosophers"; author of *Archives d'un procès Klaus Barbie* (1987).

91

London Charter. Document that prepared Nuremberg War Crimes Trials by distinguishing among the various "counts" — "war crimes," "crimes against humanity," etc.

Losey, Joseph (b. 1909). American filmmaker living in exile in Europe since the McCarthy years. His *The Boy with Green Hair* (1948) is an allegory about a war orphan who is rejected by society when his hair turns color.

Mann, Thomas (1875–1955). German novelist, author of *Death in Venice* (1910) and *The Magic Mountain* (1924). A German nationalist during in World War I, he rejected Nazism and immigrated to the United States in 1938.

M'Bemba, Jean-Martin. Congolese lawyer, member of Barbie defense team.

Metamorphosis, The. Novel by Franz Kafka in which Gregor Samsa, a traveling salesman, awakens one morning as an insect; considered Kafka's finest work. Has been read as everything from a religious allegory to a psychoanalytic case history.

Montesquieu (1689–1755). French philosopher and writer. His *Esprit des lois* was an effort to show how the varying conditions of human experience generate both written and unwritten laws.

Moulin, Jean (1899–1943). French prefect of Chartres; resigned from the Vichy government after refusing to sign a German document and accusing German soldiers of atrocities in massacring Senegalese French troops. Joined DeGaulle; charged by him with unifying the French Resistance. Betrayed to the Germans and died of torture in 1943.

Natzweiler-Struthof camp. Alsatian concentration camp that held mostly Jews and French Resistance fighters. Inmates were used as slave labor and for medical experiments; about twenty-five thousand people died there.

Noguères, Henri (b. 1916). Prosecuting attorney at Barbie trial representing the League of the Rights of Man (one of the *parties civiles*).

Nuremberg. Site of war crimes trials held by the Allies after World War II to try Nazi war criminals; an International Military Tribunal tried twenty-one Nazis in person from November 1945 to October 1946.

Patočka, Jan (1907–1977). Czech philosopher (student of Husserl); spokesman (with Vaclav Havel and Jiri Hajek) for the Charter 77 human rights manifesto; died in 1977 following an interrogation by the interior ministry.

Péguy, Charles (1873–1914). French writer and patriot; supporter of Dreyfus; founder of the *Cahiers de la Quinzaine*. His thinking evolved toward a "Catholic socialist mysticism."

Pol Pot (b. 1926). Cambodian leader; active in the 1940s in anti-French resistance under Ho Chi-Minh; became leader of the Khmer Rouge guerrillas in the 1970s. Responsible for the murder of three million civilians in the "killing fields" during his political regime from April 1975 to January 1979; in 1978 a Cambodian court sentenced him to death in absentia after finding him guilty of genocide.

Ravensbruck. Concentration camp fifty miles north of Berlin, established in 1938; held women. Liberated by the Allies in April 1945.

Revisionism. Refers to crank theories denying the fact of the Holocaust; also known, in France, as negationism. *See also* Le Pen.

Ricoeur, Paul (b. 1913). French philosopher and critic, known for his work in hermeneutic theory.

Riss, Christian. French magistrate originally charged with investigating the Barbie file. Decided against prosecuting Barbie for actions against Resistance fighters. A court of appeals overturned his decision.

Rosenberg, Alfred (1893–1946). Leading proponent of National Socialist ideology and author of *The Myth of the Twentieth Century,* the Nazi bible along with *Mein Kampf.* Reich minister for Eastern Occupied Territories; set up task force to loot art treasures from conquered areas; supervised slave labor and extermination. Executed by hanging.

Sabra and Shatila. Two Palestinian camps on the outskirts of Beirut where a massacre perpetrated by the Lebanese Christian militia took place on September 20, 1982, under the gaze of the Israeli army. The television reports were followed by international outrage and protests in Israel. A government investigation (February 1983) provoked the resignation of Ariel Sharon as Israeli Defense Minister.

Servatius, Robert. Tax and business lawyer from Cologne; defended Karl Brandt (Hitler's physician and chief of the euthenasia program) at Nuremberg and Adolf Eichmann at his 1961 Jerusalem trial.

Sétif, Algeria. Location of May 8, 1945 revolt that occurred when local police fired upon Algerians parading in the streets in celebration of the Allied victory; disturbances spread to other parts of Algeria, resulting in a repression by French military, including bombing and shelling.

Shoah. See Lanzmann, Claude.

Steiner, Jean-François (b. 1938). Author of a book on the

1943 Treblinka massacre, *Treblinka* (Paris: Fayard, 1966); the book's preface is by Simone de Beauvoir. *See also* Treblinka.

Streicher, Julius (1885–1946).   Anti-Semitic propagandist. Called for extermination of Jews in the eastern territories. Sentenced to death for crimes against humanity.

Struthof.   *See* Natzweiler-Struthof.

Treaty of Versailles.   Treaty signed June 28, 1919, that ended World War I and had immense consequences for Franco-German relations. Stipulated the return of Alsace Lorraine to France, the reduction of Germany's army, and the payment of war reparations for damage done to civilian populations. Included a war guilt clause in which Germany would accept responsibility for the war.

Treblinka.   Extermination camp in Poland at which eighty thousand prisoners were gassed in "showers" during the six months preceding the spring of 1942. On August 2, 1943, prisoners rushed the guards with hand grenades and rifles stolen from the camp arsenals; one hundred and fifty to two hundred of the seven hundred inmates escaped, but all but twelve of them were hunted down. Knowledge of the Treblinka revolt was responsible in part for the Warsaw ghetto uprising.

Truche, Pierre (b. 1930).   Chief prosecutor at the Barbie trial; requested the sentence of life in prison for Barbie.

UGIF (Union générale des israélites de France).   Official Vichy organization representing the Jewish community during the Occupation; charged with aiding and abetting the deportations.

Valéry, Paul (1871–1945).   French poet, essayist, and critic, best known for *An Evening with Mr. Teste* (1896) and *The Young Fate* (1917).

Veil, Simone (b. 1927). French Jew, survivor of Auschwitz and Bergen-Belsen. French minister of health, 1974–79; president of the European Parliament, 1979–82.

Vergès, Jacques (b. 1925). French lawyer born in Thailand of Vietnamese-French parentage; primary defense lawyer for Barbie.

Wannsee Conference. Held in a Berlin suburb on January 20, 1942, and attended by fifteen leading Nazi bureaucrats; it was at this conference that the Final Solution, which determined to exterminate the Jews, was adopted.

Index